MATTHEW ARNOLD

MATTHEW ARNOLD

BY

GEORGE *E. B.* SAINTSBURY

PROFESSOR OF RHETORIC AND ENGLISH LITERATURE IN THE
UNIVERSITY OF EDINBURGH

NEW YORK / RUSSELL & RUSSELL

PR
4023
S3
1967

FIRST PUBLISHED IN 1899
REISSUED, 1967, BY RUSSELL & RUSSELL
A DIVISION OF ATHENEUM HOUSE, INC.
L. C. CATALOG CARD NO: 66-27143
PRINTED IN THE UNITED STATES OF AMERICA

PREFACE.

MR MATTHEW ARNOLD, like other good men
of our times, disliked the idea of being made
the subject of a regular biography; and the
only official and authoritative sources of information as to the details of his life are the *Letters*
published by his family, under the editorship
of Mr G. W. E. Russell (2 vols., London, 1895).[1]
To these, therefore, it seems to be a duty to
confine oneself, as far as such details are concerned, save as regards a very few additional
facts which are public property. But very
few more facts can really be wanted except
by curiosity; for in the life of no recent person
of distinction did things literary play so large
a part as in Mr Arnold's: of no one could it

[1] Mr Arthur Galton's *Matthew Arnold* (London, 1897) adds a
few pleasant notes, chiefly about dachshunds.

be said with so much truth that, family affec-
tions and necessary avocations apart, he was
totus in illis. And these things we have in
abundance.[1] If the following pages seem to dis-
cuss them too minutely, it can only be pleaded
that those to whom it seems so are hardly in
sympathy with Matthew Arnold himself. And
if the discussion seems to any one too often
to take the form of a critical examination,
let him remember Mr Arnold's own words
in comparing the treatment of Milton by
Macaulay and by M. Scherer :—

  "Whoever comes to the *Essay on Milton* with the
desire to get at the real truth about Milton, whether
as a man or a poet, will feel that the essay in nowise
helps him. A reader who only wants rhetoric, a reader
who wants a panegyric on Milton, a panegyric on the
Puritans, will find what he wants. A reader who wants
criticism will be disappointed."

I have endeavoured, in dealing with the master
of all English critics in the latter half of the
nineteenth century, to "help the reader who wants
criticism."

  [1] It is impossible, in dealing with them, to be too grateful to Mr
T. B. Smart's *Bibliography of Matthew Arnold* (London, 1892), a
most craftsmanlike piece of work.

CONTENTS.

MATTHEW ARNOLD.

CHAPTER I.

LIFE TILL MARRIAGE, AND WORK TILL THE PUBLICATION OF THE *POEMS* OF 1853.

EVEN those who are by no means greedy of details as to the biography of authors, may without inconsistency regret that Matthew Arnold's *Letters* do not begin till he was just five-and-twenty. And then they are not copious, telling us in particular next to nothing about his literary work (which is, later, their constant subject) till he was past thirty. We could spare schoolboy letters, which, though often interesting, are pretty identical, save when written by little prigs. But the letters of an undergraduate — especially when the person is Matthew Arnold, and the University the Oxford of the years 1841-45 — ought to be not a little symptomatic, not a little illuminative. We might have learnt from them something more than we know at present about the genesis and early stages of that not entirely comprehensible or classifiable form of Liberalism in matters political, ecclesiastical, and general which, with a kind of altered Voltairian touch, attended his Conservatism in literature. Moreover, it is a real loss that we have scarcely anything from his own pen about his poems before *Sohrab and Rustum* — that is to say, about the great majority of the best of them. By the time at which we have full and frequent commentaries on himself, he is a married man, a harnessed and hard-working inspector of schools, feeling himself too busy for poetry, not as yet tempted by promptings within or invitations from without to betake himself to critical prose in any quantity or variety. Indeed, by a not much more than allowable hyperbole, we may say that we start with the book of his poetry all but shut, and the book of his prose all but unopened.

We must therefore make what we can of the subject, and of course a great deal more is to be made in such a case of the work than of the life. The facts of the latter are but scanty. Matthew Arnold, as all the world knows, was the son — the eldest son — of the famous Dr (Thomas) Arnold, Headmaster of Rugby, and Regius Professor of Modern History at Oxford, where he had earlier been a Fellow of Oriel. Dr Arnold survives in the general memory now chiefly by virtue of his head-mastership, which was really a remarkable one, whatever

distinction it may owe to the loyalty of such a group
of pupils as his son, Dean Stanley, Clough, "Tom
Brown" Hughes, and others.   But he was, if not
positively great, a notable and influential person in
many ways.   As a historian he was alert and intelligent, though perhaps too much under the influence
of that subtlest and most dangerous kind of "popular
breeze" which persuades those on whom it blows
that they are sailing not with but away from the
vulgar.   As a scholar he was ingenious, if not very
erudite or deep.   He was really a master, and has
been thought by some good judges a great master, of
that admirable late Georgian academic style of English
prose, which is almost the equal of the greatest.   But
he was, if not exactly *cupidus novarum rerum* in Church
and State, very ready to entertain them ; he was curiously deficient in logic ; and though the religious sense
was strong in him, he held, and transmitted to his
son, the heresy—the foundation of all heresies—that
religion is something that you can "bespeak," that you
can select and arrange to your own taste ; that it is
not "to take or to leave" at your peril and as it
offers itself.

On August 11, 1820, Dr Arnold married Mary Pen-
rose, and as he had devoted his teaching energies, which
were early developed, not to school or university work,
but to the taking of private pupils at Laleham on the
Thames, between Staines and Chertsey, their eldest
son was born there, on Christmas Eve, 1822.   He

was always enthusiastic about the Thames valley, though not more so than it deserves, and in his very earliest letter (January 2, 1848) we find record of a visit, when he found "the stream with the old volume, width, shine, rapid fulness, 'kempshott,'[1] and swans, unchanged and unequalled." He was only six years old when his father was elected to the head-mastership of Rugby; he was educated in his early years at his birthplace, where an uncle, the Rev. John Buckland, carried on the establishment, and at the age of fourteen he was sent to Winchester, his father's school. Here he only remained a year, and entered Rugby in August 1837. He remained there for four years, obtaining an open Balliol scholarship in 1840, though he did not go up till October 1841. In 1840 he had also gained the prize for poetry at Rugby itself with *Alaric at Rome*, a piece which was immediately printed, but never reprinted by its author, though it is now easily obtainable in the 1896 edition of those poems of his which fell out of copyright at the seven years after his death.

It is an observation seldom falsified, that such exercises, by poets of the higher class, display neither their special characteristics, nor any special characteristics at

---

[1] The editor glosses this variously spelt and etymologically puzzling word "landing-stage." But unless I mistake, a "kemp-shott," "campshed," or "campshedding" is not a landing-stage (though it helps to make one) so much as a river-wall of stakes and planks, put to guard the bank against floods, the wash of barges, &c.

all. Matthew Arnold's was not one of the exceptions. It is very much better than most school prize poems : it shows the critical and scholarly character of the writer with very fair foreshadowing ; but it does not foreshadow his poetry in the very least. It is quite free from the usual formal faults of a boy's verse, except some evidences of a deficient ear, especially for rhyme ("full" and "beautiful," "palaces" and "days"). It manages a rather difficult metre (the sixain rhymed *ababcc* and ending with an Alexandrine) without too much of the monotony which is its special danger. And some of the tricks which the boy-poet has caught are interesting and abode with him, such as the *anadiplosis*—

> "Yes, there are stories registered on high,
> Yes, there are stains Time's fingers cannot blot";

in which kind he was to produce some years later the matchless

> "Still nursing the unconquerable hope,
> Still clutching the inviolable shade,"

of the *Scholar - Gipsy*. On the whole, the thing is correct but colourless ; even its melancholy is probably mere Byronism, and has nothing directly to do with the later quality of *Dover Beach* and *Poor Matthias*.

Of Mr Arnold's undergraduate years we have unluckily but little authentic record, and, as has been said, not one letter. The most interesting evidence comes from Principal Shairp's well - known lines in

Balliol Scholars, 1840-1843, written, or at least published, many years later, in 1873 :—

> " The one wide-welcomed for a father's fame,
>   Entered with free bold step that seemed to claim
>   Fame for himself, nor on another lean.
>
> So full of power, yet blithe and debonair,
>   Rallying his friends with pleasant banter gay,
> Or half a-dream chaunting with jaunty air
>   Great words of Goethe, catch of Béranger,
> We see the banter sparkle in his prose,
> But knew not then the undertone that flows
>   So calmly sad, through all his stately lay." [1]

Like some other persons of much distinction, and a
great many of little or none, he "missed his first,"
in December 1844 ; and though he obtained, three
months later, the consolation prize of a Fellowship (at
Oriel, too), he made no post-graduate stay of any
length at the university. The then very general,
though even then not universal, necessity of taking
orders before very long would probably in any case
have sent him wandering ; for it is clear from the
first that his bent was hopelessly anti-clerical, and he
was not merely too honest, but much too proud a
man, to consent to be put in one of the priests'
offices for a morsel of bread. It may well be doubted
—though he felt and expressed not merely in splendid
passages of prose and verse for public perusal, but in
private letters quite towards the close of his life, that

---

[1] *Glen Desseray and other Poems.* By John Campbell Shairp.
London, 1888. P. 218.

passionate attachment which Oxford more than any other place of the kind inspires — whether he would have been long at home there as a resident.   For the place has at once a certain republicanism and a certain tyranny about its idea, which could not wholly suit the aspiring and restless spirit of the author of *Switzerland.*   None of her sons is important to Oxford — the meanest of them has in his sonship the same quality as the greatest.   Now it was very much at Mr Arnold's heart to be important, and he was not eager to impart or share his qualities.

However this may be, there were ample reasons why he should leave the fold.   The Bar (though he was actually called and for many years went circuit as Marshal to his father-in-law, Mr Justice Wightman) would have suited him, in practice if not in principle, even less than the Church ; and he had no scientific leanings except a taste for botany.   Although the constantly renewed cries for some not clearly defined system of public support for men of letters are, as a rule, absurd, there is no doubt that Mr Arnold was the very man for a sinecure, and would have justified the existence of Pipe or Hanaper to all reasonable men.   But his political friends had done away with nearly all such things, and no one of the very few that remained fell to his lot. His father had died in 1842, but the son served a short apprenticeship to school-teaching at Rugby, then became private secretary to Lord Lansdowne, the President of the Council (it is now that we first meet him as

an epistoler), and early in 1851 was appointed by his
chief to an inspectorship of schools.   Having now a
livelihood, he married, in June of that year, Frances
Lucy Wightman, daughter of a judge of the Queen's
Bench.   Their first child, Thomas, was born on July 6,
1852, and Mr Arnold was now completely estated in
the three positions of husband, father, and inspector of
schools, which occupied — to his great delight in the
first two cases, not quite so in the third—most of his life
that was not given to literature.   Some not ungenerous
but perhaps rather unnecessary indignation has been
spent upon his "drudgery" and its scanty rewards.   It
is enough to say that few men can arrange at their
pleasure the quantity and quality of their work, and
that not every man, even of genius, has had his bread-
and-butter secured for life at eight-and-twenty.

But in the ten or twelve years which had passed since
Alaric at Rome, literature itself had been by no means
neglected, and in another twelvemonth after the birth of
his first-born, Matthew Arnold had practically established
his claim as a poet by utterances to which he made comparatively small additions later, though more than half
his life was yet to run.   And he had issued one prose
exercise in criticism, of such solidity and force as had not
been shown by any poet since Dryden, except Coleridge.

These documents can hardly be said to include the
Newdigate poem (*Cromwell*) of 1843 : they consist of
The Strayed Reveller and other Poems, by "A.," 1849 ;
Empedocles on Etna, and other Poems, [still] by "A.,"

1852; and *Poems* by Matthew Arnold, a new edition, 1853—the third consisting of the contents of the two earlier, with *Empedocles* and a few minor things omitted, but with very important additions, including *Sohrab and Rustum*, *The Church of Brou*, *Requiescat*, and *The Scholar-Gipsy*. The contents of all three must be carefully considered, and the consideration may be prefaced by a few words on *Cromwell*.

This ἀγώνισμα, like the other, Mr Arnold never included in any collection of his work ; but it was printed at Oxford in the year of its success, and again at the same place, separately or with other prize poems, in 1846, 1863, and 1891. It may also be found in the useful non-copyright edition above referred to. Couched in the consecrated couplet, but not as of old limited to fifty lines, it is "good rhymes," as the elder Mr Pope used to say to the younger ; but a prudent taster would perhaps have abstained, even more carefully than in the case of the *Alaric*, from predicting a real poet in the author. It is probably better than six Newdigates out of seven at least, but it has no distinction. The young, but not so very young, poet—he was as old as Tennyson when he produced his unequal but wonderful first volume—begins by borrowing Wordsworth's two voices of the mountain and the sea, shows some impression here and there from Tennyson's own master-issue, the great collection of 1842, which had appeared a year before, ventures on an Alexandrine—

" Between the barren mountains and the stormy sea "—

which comes as a pleasant relief, and displays more than once (as he did afterwards in *Tristram and Iseult*) an uncertain but by no means infelicitous variety of couplet which he never fully or fairly worked out, but left for Mr William Morris to employ with success many years later. Otherwise the thing is good, but negligible. It would have taken an extremely strong competition, or an extremely incompetent examiner, to deprive it of the prize ; but he must have been a sanguine man who, in giving the author that prize, expected to receive from him returns of poetry.

Yet they came. If we did not know that the middle of this century was one of the nadirs of English [1] criticism, and if we did not know further that even good critics often go strangely wrong both in praise and in blame of new verse, it would be most surprising that *The Strayed Reveller* volume should have attracted so little attention. It is full of faults, but that is part of

---

[1] This statement may seem too sweeping, especially as there is neither room nor occasion for justifying it fully. Let us only indicate, as among the heads of such a justification, the following sins of English criticism between 1840-1860,—the slow and reluctant acceptance even of Tennyson, even of Thackeray ; the obstinate refusal to give Browning, even after *Bells and Pomegranates*, a fair hearing ; the recalcitrance to Carlyle among the elder, and Mr Ruskin among the younger, innovators in prose ; the rejection of a book of erratic genius like *Lavengro ;* the ignoring of work of such combined intrinsic beauty and historic importance as *The Defence of Guenevere* and FitzGerald's *Omar Khayyam.* For a sort of quintessence of literary Philistinism, see the advice of Richard Ford (himself no Philistine) to George Borrow, in Professor Knapp's *Life* of the latter, i. 387.

the beauty of it. Some of these faults are those which, persevering, prevented Mr Arnold from attaining a higher position than he actually holds in poetry ; but no critic could know that. There is nothing here worse, or more necessarily fatal, than many things in Tennyson's 1830 and 1832 collections : he overwent those, so might Mr Arnold have overgone these. And the promise—nay, the performance—is such as had been seen in no verse save Tennyson's, and the almost unnoticed Browning's, for some thirty years. The title-poem, though it should have pleased even a severe judge, might have aroused uncomfortable doubts even in an amiable one. In the first place, its rhymelessness is a caprice, a will-worship. Except blank verse, every rhymeless metre in English has on it the curse of the *tour de force*, of the acrobatic. Campion and Collins, Southey and Shelley, have done great things in it ; but neither *Rose-cheeked Laura* nor *Evening*, neither the great things in *Thalaba* nor the great things in *Queen Mab*, can escape the charge of being caprices. And caprice, as some have held, is the eternal enemy of art.

But the caprice of *The Strayed Reveller* does not cease with its rhymelessness. The rhythm and the line-division are also studiously odd, unnatural, paradoxical. Except for the " poetic diction " of putting " Goddess " after " Circe " instead of before it, the first stave is merely a prose sentence, of strictly prosaic though not inharmonious rhythm. But in this stave there is no instance of the strangest peculiarity, and what seems to some the worst fault of the piece, the profusion of broken-up decasyllables, which sometimes suggest a very "corrupt" manuscript, or a passage of that singular stuff in the Caroline dramatists which is neither blank verse, nor any other, nor prose.   Here are a few out of many instances—

> " Is it, then, evening
> So soon ?   [*I see the night-dews
> Clustered in thick beads*], dim," etc.
>
> .   .   .   .   .
>
> ["*When the white dawn first
> Through the rough fir-planks.*"]
>
> .   .   .   .   .
>
> ["*Thanks, gracious One !
> Ah ! the sweet fumes again.*"]
>
> .   .   .   .   .
>
> ["*They see the Centaurs
> In the upper glens.*"]

One could treble these—indeed in one instance (the sketch of the Indian) the entire stanza of *eleven* lines, by the insertion of one "and" only, becomes a smooth blank - verse piece of *seven*, two of which are indeed hemistichs, and three "weak-ended," but only such as are frequent in Shakespeare—

> " They see the Indian drifting, knife in hand,
> His frail boat moored to a floating isle—thick-matted
> With large-leaved [*and*] low-creeping melon-plants
> And the dark cucumber.
> He reaps and stows them, drifting, drifting : round him,
> Round his green harvest-plot, flow the cool lake-waves,
> The mountains ring them. "

Nor, perhaps, though the poem is a pretty one, will it stand criticism of a different kind much better.   Such

mighty personages as Ulysses and Circe are scarcely
wanted as mere bystanders and " supers " to an imaginative young gentleman who enumerates, somewhat
promiscuously, a few of the possible visions of the Gods.
There is neither classical, nor romantic, nor logical
justification for any such mild effect of the dread Wine
of Circe : and one is driven to the conclusion that the
author chiefly wanted a frame, after his own fashion, for
a set of disconnected vignettes like those of Tennyson's
Palace of Art and *Dream of Fair Women*.

But if the title poem is vulnerable, there is plenty of
compensation.   The opening sonnet—

" Two lessons, Nature, let me learn of thee "—

is perhaps rather learnt from Wordsworth, yet it does
not fail to strike the note which fairly differentiates
the Arnoldian variety of Wordsworthianism—the note
which rings from *Resignation* to *Poor Matthias*, and
which is a very curious cross between two things that
at first sight may seem unmarriageable, the Wordsworthian enthusiasm and the Byronic despair.   But
of this [1] more when we have had more of its examples
before us.   The second piece in the volume must, or
should, have struck — for there is very little evidence
that it did strike—readers of the volume as something
at once considerable and, in no small measure, new.
Mycerinus, a piece of some 120 lines or so, in thirteen
six-line stanzas and a blank-verse *coda*, is one of those

―――――――――

[1] This "undertone," as Mr Shairp calls it.

characteristic poems of this century, which are neither mere "copies of verses," mere occasional pieces, nor substantive compositions of the old kind, with at least an attempt at a beginning, middle, and end. They attempt rather situations than stories, rather facets than complete bodies of thought, or description, or character. They supply an obvious way of escape for the Romantic tendency which does not wish to break wholly with classical tradition ; and above all, they admit of indulgence in that immense *variety* which seems to have become one of the chief devices of modern art, attempting the compliances necessary to gratify modern taste.

The Herodotean anecdote of the Egyptian King Mycerinus, his indignation at the sentence of death in six years as a recompense for his just rule, and his device of lengthening his days by revelling all night, is neither an unpromising nor a wholly promising subject. The foolish good sense of Mr Toots would probably observe—and justly—that before six years, or six months, or even six days were over, King Mycerinus must have got very sleepy ; and the philosophic mind would certainly recall the parallel of Cleobis and Biton as to the best gift for man. Mr Arnold, however, draws no direct moral. The stanza-part of the poem, the king's expostulation, contains very fine poetry, and "the note" rings again throughout it, especially in the couplet—

> " And prayers, and gifts, and tears, are fruitless all,
> *And the night waxes, and the shadows fall.*"

The blank-verse tail-piece is finer still in execution; it is, with the still finer companion-*coda* of *Sohrab and Rustum*, the author's masterpiece in the kind, and it is, like that, an early and consummate example of Mr Arnold's favourite device of finishing without a finish, of "playing out the audience," so to speak, with something healing and reconciling, description, simile, what not, to relieve the strain of his generally sad philosophy and his often melancholy themes.

One may less admire, despite its famous and often-quoted line,

"Who saw life steadily, and saw it whole,"

the sonnet *To a Friend*, praising Homer and Epictetus and Sophocles, for it seems to some to have a smatch of priggishness.   Nor am I one of those who think very highly of the much longer *Sick King in Bokhara* which (with a fragment of an *Antigone*, whereof more hereafter) follows, as this sonnet precedes, *The Strayed Reveller* itself.   There is "the note," again, and I dare-say the orientalism has the exactness of colour on which, as we know from the *Letters*, Mr Arnold prided himself.   Yet the handling of the piece seems to me prolix and uncertain, and the drift either very obscure or somewhat unimportant.   But about the *Shakespeare* sonnet which follows there can be no controversy among the competent.   "Almost adequate" is in such a case the highest praise; and it must be given.

The companions of this sonnet are respectable, but

do not deserve much warmer words ; and then we turn
to a style of poem remarkably different from anything
which the author had yet published and from most of
his subsequent work.   It is not unnoteworthy that the
batch of poems called in the later collected editions
Switzerland, and completed at last by the piece called
On the Terrace at Berne, appeared originally piecemeal,
and with no indication of connection.   The first of
its numbers is here, *To my Friends who Ridiculed a
Tender Leave - taking*.   It applies both the note of
thought which has been indicated, and the quality of
style which had already disengaged itself, to the com-
monest — the greatest — theme of poetry, but to one
which this poet had not yet tried — to Love.   Let
it be remembered that the thought has the cast of
a strictly pessimist quietism — that the style aims, if
it aims at any single thing, at the reproduction of the
simpler side of classicalism, at an almost prim and
quakerish *elegance*, a sort of childlike grace.   There
is, however, by no means any great austerity in the
tone : on the contrary, the refrain (altered later)—

> " Ere the parting kiss be dry,
> Quick ! thy tablets, Memory ! "—

approaches the luscious.   It is not easy to decide, and
it is perhaps in both senses impertinent to speculate,
whether the " Marguerite " (whose La Tour-like portrait
is drawn in this piece with such relish, and who is so
philosophically left to her fate by her lover on the

Terrace at Berne later) had any live original. She seems a little more human in some ways than most of those cloud-Junos of the poets, the heroines of sonnet-sequence and song-string. She herself has a distinct touch of philosophy, anticipating with nonchalant resignation the year's severance, and with equally nonchalant anticipation the time when

> "Some day next year I shall be,
> Entering heedless, kissed by thee."

Her wooer paints her with gusto, but scarcely with ardour ; and ends with the boding note—

> "Yet, if little stays with man,
> Ah ! retain we all we can !"—

seeming to be at least as doubtful of his own constancy as of hers. Nor do we meet her again in the volume. The well-known complementary pieces which make up *Switzerland* were either not written, or held back.

The inferior but interesting *Modern Sappho*, almost the poet's only experiment in " Moore-ish " method and melody—

"They are gone—all is still !   Foolish heart, dost thou quiver ? "—

is a curiosity rather than anything else. The style is ill suited to the thought ; besides, Matthew Arnold, a master at times of blank verse, and of the statelier stanza, was less often an adept at the lighter and more rushing lyrical measures. He is infinitely more at home in the beautiful *New Sirens*, which, for what reason it is difficult to discover, he never reprinted till many years later, partly at Mr Swinburne's most judicious suggestion.   The scheme is trochaic, and Mr Arnold (deriving beyond all doubt inspiration from Keats) was happier than most poets with that charming but difficult foot.   The note is the old one of yearning rather than passionate melancholy, applied in a new way and put most clearly, though by no means most poetically, in the lines—

> "Can men worship the wan features,
> The sunk eyes, the wailing tone,
> Of unsphered, discrowned creatures,
> Souls as little godlike as their own?"

The answer is, "No," of course; but, as some one informed Mr Arnold many years later, we knew that before, and it is distressing to be told it, as we are a little later, with a rhyme of "dawning" and "morning." Yet the poem is a very beautiful one—in some ways the equal of its author's best up to this time; at least he had yet done nothing except the *Shakespeare* sonnet equal to the splendid stanza beginning—

> "And we too, from upland valleys;"

and the cry of the repentant sirens, punished as they had sinned—

> "'Come,' you say, 'the hours are dreary.'"

Yet the strong Tennysonian influence (which the poet rather ungraciously kicked against in his criticism) shows itself here also ; and we know perfectly well that the good lines—

> " When the first *rose* flush was steeping
> All the frore peak's *awful* crown "—

are but an unconscious reminiscence of the great ones—

> "And on the glimmering summit far withdrawn,
> God made himself an *awful rose* of dawn."

He kept this level, though here following not Tennyson or Keats but Shelley, in the three ambitious and elaborate lyrics, *The Voice*, *To Fausta*, and *Stagirius*, fine things, if somehow a little suggestive of inability on their author's part fully to meet the demands of the forms he attempts—"the note," in short, expressed practically as well as in theory. *Stagirius* in particular wants but a very little to be a perfect expression of the obstinate questionings of the century ; and yet wanting a little, it wants so much !   Others, *To a Gipsy Child* and *The Hayswater Boat* (Mr Arnold never reprinted this), are but faint Wordsworthian echoes ; and thus we come to *The Forsaken Merman.*

It is, I believe, not so "correct" as it once was to admire this ; but I confess indocility to correctness, at least the correctness which varies with fashion.   *The Forsaken Merman* is not a perfect poem—it has *longueurs*, though it is not long ; it has those inadequacies, those incompetences of expression, which are so oddly characteristic of its author ; and his elaborate simplicity, though more at home here than in some other places,

occasionally gives a dissonance. But it is a great poem
—one by itself, one which finds and keeps its own place
in the foreordained gallery or museum, with which
every true lover of poetry is provided, though he in-
herits it by degrees. No one, I suppose, will deny its
pathos ; I should be sorry for any one who fails to perceive its beauty. The brief picture of the land, and
the fuller one of the sea, and that (more elaborate still)
of the occupations of the fugitive, all have their own
charm. But the triumph of the piece is in one of those
metrical *coups* which give the triumph of all the greatest
poetry, in the sudden change from the slower move-
ments of the earlier stanzas or strophes to the quicker
sweep of the famous conclusion—

> " The salt tide rolls seaward,
>   Lights shine from the town "—

to

> " She left lonely for ever
>   The kings of the sea."

Here the poet's poetry has come to its own.

In Utrumque Paratus sounds the note again, and
has one exceedingly fine stanza :—

> " Thin, thin the pleasant human noises grow,
>   And faint the city gleams;
> Rare the lone pastoral huts—marvel not thou !
> The solemn peaks but to the stars are known,
> But to the stars, and the cold lunar beams ;
> Alone the sun arises, and alone
>   Spring the great streams."

But *Resignation*, the last poem in the book, goes far

higher.   Again, it is too long; and, as is not the
case in the *Merman*, or even in *The Strayed Reveller*
itself, the *general* drift of the poem, the allegory (if
it be an allegory) of the two treadings of "the self-
same road" with Fausta and so forth, is unnecessarily
obscure, and does not tempt one to spend much
trouble in penetrating its obscurity.   But the splendid
passage beginning—

> " The Poet to whose mighty heart,"

and ending—

> " His sad lucidity of soul,"

has far more interest than concerns the mere introduction, in this last line itself, of one of the famous
Arnoldian catchwords of later years.   It has far
more than lies even in its repetition, with fuller de-
tail, of what has been called the author's main poetic
note of half - melancholy contemplation of life.   It
has, once more, the interest of *poetry*—of poetical
presentation, which is independent of any subject or
intention, which is capable of being adapted perhaps
to all, certainly to most, which lies in form, in sound,
in metre, in imagery, in language, in suggestion —
rather than in matter, in sense, in definite purpose
or scheme.

It is one of the heaviest indictments against the
criticism of the mid-nineteenth century that this remarkable book — the most remarkable first book of
verse that appeared between Tennyson's and Brown-

ing's in the early thirties and *The Defence of Guenevere* in 1858 — seems to have attracted next to no
notice at all. It received neither the ungenerous and
purblind, though not wholly unjust, abuse which in
the long - run did so much good to Tennyson himself, nor the absurd and pernicious bleatings of praise
which have greeted certain novices of late years. It
seems to have been simply let alone, or else made
the subject of quite insignificant comments.

In the same year (1849) Mr Arnold was represented in the *Examiner* of July 21 by a sonnet to
the Hungarian nation, which he never included in
any book, and which remained peacefully in the dust-
bin till a reference in his *Letters* quite recently set
the ruthless reprinter on its track. Except for an
ending, itself not very good, the thing is quite valueless : the author himself says to his mother, "it is
not worth much." And three years passed before he
followed up his first volume with a second, which
should still more clearly have warned the intelligent
critic that here was somebody, though such a critic
would not have been guilty of undue hedging if he
had professed himself still unable to decide whether
a new great poet had arisen or not.

This volume was *Empedocles on Etna and other
Poems*, [still] *By A.* London : Fellowes, 1852. It
contained two attempts — the title - piece and *Tristram and Iseult* — much longer and more ambitious
than anything that the poet had yet done, and thirty-

three smaller poems, of which two — *Destiny* and
Courage — were never reprinted.   It was again very
unequal — perhaps more so than the earlier volume,
though it went higher and oftener high.   But the
author became dissatisfied with it very shortly after
its appearance in the month of October, and withdrew
it when, as is said, less than fifty copies had been sold.

One may perhaps not impertinently doubt whether the
critical reason, *v. infra*—in itself a just and penetrating one, as well as admirably expressed—which, in the
Preface of the 1853 collection, the poet gave for its
exclusion (save in very small part) from that volume
tells the whole truth.   At any rate, I think most
good judges quarrel with *Empedocles*, not because the
situation is unmanageable, but because the poet has
not managed it.   The contrast, in dramatic trio, of
the world-worn and disappointed philosopher, the practical and rather prosaic physician, and the fresh gifts
and unspoilt gusto of the youthful poet, is neither
impossible nor unpromising.   Perhaps, as a situation,
it is a little nearer than Mr Arnold quite knew to
that of *Paracelsus*, and it is handled with less force,
if with more clearness, than Browning's piece.   But
one does not know what is more amiss with it than
is amiss with most of its author's longer pieces —
namely, that neither story nor character - drawing was
his *forte*, that the dialogue is too colourless, and that
though the description is often charming, it is seldom
masterly.   As before, there are jarring rhymes —

" school " and " oracle," " Faun " and " scorn." Empedocles himself is sometimes dreadfully tedious ; but
the part of Callicles throughout is lavishly poetical.
Not merely the show passages—that which the Roman
father,

> " Though young, intolerab'y severe,"

saved from banishment and retained by itself in the 1853
volume, as *Cadmus and Harmonia,* and the beautiful
lyrical close,—but the picture of the highest wooded
glen on Etna, and the Flaying of Marsyas, are delightful things.

Tristram and Iseult, with fewer good patches, has a
greater technical interest. It is only one, but it is the
most remarkable, of the places where we perceive in Mr
Arnold one of the most curious of the notes of transi-
tion-poets. They will not frankly follow another's metrical form, and they cannot strike out a new one for
themselves. In this piece the author—most attractively
to the critic, if not always quite satisfactorily to the
reader—makes for, and flits about, half-a-dozen different
forms of verse. Now it is the equivalenced octosyllable
of the Coleridgean stamp rather than of Scott's or
Byron's ; now trochaic decasyllables of a rather rococo
kind ; and once at least a splendid anapæstic couplet,
which catches the ear and clings to the memory for a
lifetime—

> " What voices are these on the clear night air ?
> What lights in the court ?   What steps on the stair ? "

But the most interesting experiment by far is in the

rhymed heroic, which appears fragmentarily in the first two parts and substantively in the third. The interest of this, which (one cannot but regret it) Mr Arnold did not carry further, relapsing on a stiff if stately blank verse, is not merely intrinsic, but both retrospective and prospective. It is not the ordinary "stopped" eighteenth-century couplet at all; nor the earlier one of Drayton and Daniel. It is the "enjambed," very mobile, and in the right hands admirably fluent and adaptable couplet, which William Browne and Chamberlayne practised in the early and middle seventeenth century, which Leigh Hunt revived and taught to Keats, and of which, later than Mr Arnold himself, Mr William Morris was such an admirable practitioner. Its use here is decidedly happy; and the whole of this part shows in Mr Arnold a temporary Romantic impulse, which again we cannot but regret that he did not obey. The picture-work of the earlier lines is the best he ever did. The figure of Iseult with the White Hands stands out with the right Præ-Raphaelite distinctness and charm; and the story of Merlin and Vivian, with which, in the manner so dear to him, he diverts the attention of the reader from the main topic at the end, is beautifully told. For attaching quality on something like a large scale I should put this part of *Tristram and Iseult* much above both *Sohrab and Rustum* and *Balder Dead;* but the earlier parts are not worthy of it, and the whole, like *Empedocles*, is something of a failure, though both poems afford ample consolation in passages.

The smaller pieces, however, could have saved the volume had their larger companions been very much weaker. The *Memorial Verses* on Wordsworth (published first in *Fraser*) have taken their place once for all. If they have not the poetical beauty in different ways of Carew on Donne, of Dryden on Oldham, even of Tickell upon Addison, of *Adonais* above all, of Wordsworth's own beautiful *Effusion* on the group of dead poets in 1834, they do not fall far short even in this respect. And for adequacy of meaning, not unpoetically expressed, they are almost supreme. If Mr Arnold's own unlucky and maimed definition of poetry as "a criticism of life" had been true, they would be poetry in quintessence; and, as it is, they are poetry.

Far more so is the glorious *Summer Night*, which came near the middle of the book. There is a cheering doctrine of mystical optimism which will have it that a sufficiently intense devotion to any ideal never fails of at least one moment of consummate realisation and enjoyment. Such a moment was granted to Matthew Arnold when he wrote *A Summer Night*. Whether that rather vague life-philosophy of his, that erection of a melancholy agnosticism *plus* asceticism into a creed, was anything more than a not ungraceful or undignified will-worship of Pride, we need not here argue out. But we have seen how faithfully the note of it rings through the verse of these years. And here it rings not only faithfully, but almost triumphantly. The

lips are touched at last : the eyes are thoroughly opened
to see what the lips shall speak : the brain almost unconsciously frames and fills the adequate and inevitable
scheme.   And, as always at these right poetic moments,
the minor felicities follow the major.   The false rhymes
are nowhere ; the imperfect phrases, the little sham
simplicities or pedantries, hide themselves ; and the poet
is free, from the splendid opening landscape through
the meditative exposition, and the fine picture of the
shipwreck, to the magnificent final invocation of the
" Clearness divine ! "

His freedom, save once, is not so unquestionably exhibited in the remarkable group of poems—the future
constituents of the *Switzerland* group, but still not
classified under any special head—which in the original volume chiefly follow *Empedocles*, with the batch
later called " Faded Leaves " to introduce them.   It
is, perhaps, if such things were worth attempting at all,
an argument for supposing some real undercurrent of
fact or feeling in them, that they are not grouped at
their first appearance, and that some of them are
perhaps designedly separated from the rest.   Even the
name " Marguerite " does not appear in *A Farewell ;*
though nobody who marked as well as read, could fail
to connect it with the *To my Friends* of the former
volume.   We are to suppose, it would appear, that
the twelvemonth has passed, and that Marguerite's anticipation of the renewed kiss is fulfilled in the first
stanzas.   But the lover's anticipation, too, is ful-

filled, though as usual not quite as he made it; he
wearies of his restless and yet unmasterful passion;
he rather muses and morals in his usual key on
the "way of a man with a maid" than complains or
repines. And then we go off for a time from Marguerite, though not exactly from Switzerland, in the
famous "*Obermann*" stanzas, a variation of the Wordsworth memorial lines, melodious, but a very little *impotent*—the English utterance of what Sainte-Beuve, I
think, called "the discouraged generation of 1850."
Now mere discouragement, except as a passing mood,
though extremely natural, is also a little contemptible—
pessimism-and-water, mere peevishness to the "fierce
indignation," mere whining compared with the great
ironic despair. As for *Consolation*, which in form as in
matter strongly resembles part of the *Strayed Reveller*, I
must say, at the risk of the charge of Philistinism, that I
cannot see why most of it should not have been printed
as prose. In fact, it would be a very bold and astonish-
ingly ingenious person who, not knowing the original,
perceived any verse-division in this—

"The bleak, stern hour, whose severe moments I would anni-
hilate, is passed by others in warmth, light, joy."

Nor perhaps can very much be said for some of
the other things. The sonnet afterwards entitled *The
World's Triumphs* is not strong; *The Second Best* is but
"a chain of extremely valuable thoughts"; *Revolution*
a conceit. *The Youth of Nature* and *The Youth of*

Man do but take up less musically the *threnos* for Wordsworth.   But *Morality* is both rhyme and poetry; *Progress* is at least rhyme; and *The Future*, though rhymeless again, is the best of all Mr Arnold's wayward-nesses of this kind.   It is, however, in the earlier division of the smaller poems—those which come between *Em-pedocles* and *Tristram*—that the interest is most concen-trated, and that the best thing—better as far as its sub-ject is concerned even than the *Summer Night*—appears. For though all does *not* depend upon the subject, yet of two poems equally good in other ways, that which has the better subject will be the better.   Here we have the bulk of the " Marguerite " or *Switzerland* poems—in other words, we leave the windy vagaries of mental in-digestion and come to the real things—Life and Love.

The River does not name any one, though the " arch eyes " identify Marguerite ; and *Excuse, Indifference*, and *Too Late* are obviously of the company.   But none of these is exactly of the first class.   We grow warmer with *On the Rhine*, containing, among other things, the good distich—

> " Eyes too expressive to be blue,
>   Too lovely to be grey " ;

on which Mr Swinburne gave a probably unconscious *scholion* as well as variation in his own—

> " Those eyes, the greenest of things blue,
>   The bluest of things grey."

The intense pathos, which the poet could rarely

"let himself go" sufficiently to reach, together with
the seventeenth-century touch which in English not
unfrequently rewards the self-sacrifice necessary to
scholarly poets in such abandonment, appears in
Longing; The Lake takes up the faint thread of story
gracefully enough; and *Parting* does the same with
more importance in a combination, sometimes very
effective, of iambic couplets and anapæstic strophes,
and with a touch of direct if not exalted nature in its
revelation of that terrible thing, retrospective jealousy,
in the lover.   Woe to the man who allows himself to
think—

> "To the lips! ah! of others
>   Those lips have been pressed,
> And others, ere I was,
>   Were clasped to that breast,"

and who does not at once exorcise the demon with
the fortunately all-potent spell of *Bocca bacciata*, and
the rest!   *Absence* and *Destiny* show him in the same
Purgatory; and it is impossible to say that he has
actually escaped in the crowning poem of the series
—the crowning-point perhaps of his poetry, the piece
beginning

> "Yes! in the sea of life enisled."

It is neither uninteresting nor unimportant that this
exquisite piece, by a man's admiration of which (for
there are some not wholly lost, who do *not* admire
it) his soundness in the Catholic Faith of poetry may
be tested, perhaps as well as by any other, has borne

more than one or two titles. It is in the 1852 volume, *To Marguerite. In returning a volume of the letters of Ortis*. In 1853 it became *Isolation*, its best name; and later it took the much less satisfactory one of *To Marguerite—continued*, being annexed to another.

Isolation is preferable for many reasons; not least because the actual Marguerite appears nowhere in the poem, and, except in the opening monosyllable, can hardly be said to be even rhetorically addressed. The poet's affection—it is scarcely passion—is there, but in transcendence : he meditates more than he feels. And that function of the riddle of the painful earth which Lucretius, thousands of years ago, put in his grim *Nequicquam !* which one of Mr Arnold's own contemporaries formulated with less magnificence and more popularity; but still with music and truth in *Strangers Yet*—here receives almost its final poetical expression. The image — the islands in the sea — is capitally projected in the first stanza; it is exquisitely amplified in the second ; the moral comes with due force in the third ; and the whole winds up with one of the great poetic phrases of the century—one of the "jewels five [literally five !] words long" of English verse—a phrase complete and final, with epithets in unerring cumulation—

"The unplumb'd, salt, estranging sea."

Human Life, no ill thing in itself, reads a little

weakly after *Isolation ;* but *Despondency* is a pretty piece of melancholy, and, with a comfortable stool, will suit a man well. In the sonnet, *When I shall be divorced*, Mr Arnold tried the Elizabethan vein with less success than in his Shakespeare piece ; and *Self - Deception* and *Lines written by a Death - Bed*, with some beauty have more monotony. The closing lines of the last are at the same time the moral of the book and the formula of the Arnoldian " note "—

> " Calm's not life's crown, though calm is well.
> 'Tis all perhaps which man acquires,
> But 'tis not what our youth desires."

Again, we remember some one's parody - remonstrance thirty years later, and again we may think that the condemnation which Mr Arnold himself was soon to pronounce upon *Empedocles* is rather disastrously far-reaching, while even this phrase is a boomerang. Musical and philosophical despair is one of the innumerable strings of the poetic lyre ; but 'tis not what our youth, or our age either, desires for a monochord.

The remarkable manifesto just referred to was not long delayed. Whatever may have been his opinion as to the reception of the two volumes "by A," he made up his mind, a year after the issue and withdrawal of the second, to put forth a third, with his name, and containing, besides a full selection from the other two, fresh specimens of the greatest importance. In the two former there had been no avowed "purpose"; here, not merely were the contents sifted on principle, the important *Empedocles* as well as some minor things being omitted : not merely did some of the new numbers, especially *Sohrab and Rustum*, directly and intentionally illustrate the poet's theories, but those theories themselves were definitely put in a *Preface*, which is the most important critical document issued in England for something like a generation, and which, as prefixed by a poet to his poetry, admits no competitors in English, except some work of Dryden's and some of Wordsworth's.

Beginning with his reasons for discarding *Empedocles*, reasons which he sums up in a sentence, famous, but too important not to require citation at least in a note,[1] he passes suddenly to the reasons which were *not* his, and of which he makes a good rhetorical starting-point for his main course.   The bad critics of that day had promulgated the doctrine, which they maintained till a time within the memory of most men who have reached middle life, though the error has since in the usual course given way to others — that "the Poet

[1] " What, then, are the situations, from the representation of which, though accurate, no poetical enjoyment can be derived ?   They are those in which the suffering finds no vent in action ; in which a continuous state of mental distress is prolonged, unrelieved by incident, hope, or resistance ; in which there is everything to be endured, nothing to be done.   In such situations there is inevitably something morbid, in the description of them something monotonous. When they occur in actual life, they are painful, not tragic ; the representation of them in poetry is painful also."

must leave the exhausted past and draw his subjects from matters of present import." This was the genuine "*Times-v.*-all-the-works-of-Thucydides" fallacy of the mid-nineteenth century, the fine flower of Cobdenism, the heartfelt motto of Philistia—as Philistia then was. For other times other Philistines, and Ekron we have always with us, ready, as it was once said, "to bestow its freedom in pinchbeck boxes" on its elect.

This error Mr Arnold has no difficulty in laying low at once; but unluckily his swashing blow carries him with it, and he falls headlong into fresh error himself. "What," he asks very well, "are the eternal objects of Poetry, among all nations and at all times?" And he answers—equally well, though not perhaps with impregnable logical completeness and accuracy—"They are actions, human actions; possessing an inherent interest in themselves, and which are to be communicated in an interesting manner by the art of the Poet." Here he tells the truth, but not the whole truth; he should have added "thoughts and feelings" to "actions," or he deprives Poetry of half her realm. But he is so far sufficient against his Harapha (for at that date there were no critical Goliaths about). Human action *does* possess an "inherent," an "eternal," poetical interest and capacity in itself. That interest, that capacity, is incapable of "exhaustion"—nay (as Mr Arnold, though with bad arguments as well as good, urges later), it is, on the whole, a likelier subject for the poet when it is old, because it is capable of being grasped and presented more certainly.   But the defender hastens to indulge in more than one of those dangerous sallies from his trenches which have been fatal to so many heroes.   He proclaims that the poet cannot "make an intrinsically inferior action equally delightful with a more excellent one by his treatment of it," forgetting that, until the action is presented, we do not know whether it is "inferior" or not.   He asks, "What modern poem presents personages as interesting as Achilles, Prometheus, Clytemnestra, Dido ?" unsuspicious, or perhaps reckless, of the fact that not a few men, who admire and know the classics quite as well as he does, will cheerfully take up his challenge at any weapons he likes to name, and with a score of instances for his quartette.   It is true that, thanks to the ineptitude of his immediate antagonists, he recovers himself not ill by cleverly selecting the respectable Hermann and Dorothea, the stagy-romantic Childe Harold, the creature called "Jocelyn," and the shadowy or scrappy personages of the *Excursion*, to match against his four.   But this is manifestly unfair. To bring Lamartine and Wordsworth in as personage-makers is only honest rhetorically (a kind of honesty on which Wamba or Launcelot Gobbo shall put the gloss for us).   Nay, even those to whom Goethe and Byron are not the ideal of modern poetry may retort that Mephistopheles—that even Faust himself—is a much more "interesting" person than the sulky invulnerable son of Thetis, while Gulnare, Parisina, and others are not much worse than Dido.   But these are mere details.

The main purpose of the *Preface* is to assert in the most emphatic manner the Aristotelian (or partly Aristotelian) doctrine that "All depends on the subject," and to connect the assertion with a further one, of which even less proof is offered, that "the Greeks understood this far better than we do," and that they were *also* the unapproachable masters of "the grand style." These positions, which, to do Mr Arnold justice, he maintained unflinchingly to his dying day, are supported, not exactly by argument, but by a great deal of ingenious and audacious illustration and variation of statement, even Shakespeare, even Keats, being arraigned for their wicked refusal to subordinate "expression" to choice and conception of subject. The merely Philistine modernism is cleverly set up again that it may be easily smitten down ; the necessity of Criticism, and of the study of the ancients in order to it, is most earnestly and convincingly championed ; and the piece ends with its other famous sentence about "the wholesome regulative laws of Poetry" and their "eternal enemy, Caprice."

As Mr Arnold's critical position will be considered as a whole later, it would be waste of time to say very much more of this first manifesto of his. It need only be observed that he might have been already, as he often was later, besought to give some little notion of what "the *grand style*" was ; that, true and sound as is much of the Preface, it is not a little exposed to the damaging retort, " Yes : this is *your* doxy, and she seems fair to you, no doubt; but so does ours seem fair to us." Moreover, the "all-depends-on-the-subject" doctrine here, as always, swerves from one fatal difficulty. If, in what pleases poetically, poetical expression is always present, while in only some of what pleases poetically is the subject at the required height, is it not illogical to rule out, as the source of the poetic pleasure, that which is always present in favour of that which is sometimes absent?

We know from the *Letters*—and we should have been able to divine without them—that *Sohrab and Rustum*, the first in order, the largest in bulk, and the most ambitious in scheme of the poems which appeared for the first time in the new volume, was written in direct exemplification of the theories of the *Preface*. The theme is old, and though not "classical" in place, is thoroughly so in its nature, being the story of a combat between a father and a son, who know not each other till too late, of the generosity of the son, of the final triumph of the father, of the *anagnorisis*, with the resignation of the vanquished and the victor's despair. The medium is blank verse, of a partly but not wholly Miltonic stamp, very carefully written, and rising at the end into a really magnificent strain, with the famous picture of "the majestic river" Oxus floating on regardless of these human woes, to where the stars

"Emerge, and shine upon the Aral Sea."

Even here, it is true, the Devil's Advocate may ask
whether this, like the *Mycerinus* close, that of *Empedocles*, and others, especially one famous thing, to
which we shall come presently, is not more of a
purple tail-patch, a "tag," a "curtain," than of a
legitimate and integral finale. It is certain that
Mr Arnold, following the Greeks in intention no
doubt, if not quite so closely as he intended, was
very fond of these "curtains"—these little rhetorical
reconciliations and soothings for the reader. But this
is the most in place of any of them, and certainly
the noblest *tirade* that its author has left.

Most of the new poems here are at a level but
a little lower than this part of *Sohrab and Rustum*,
while some of them are even above it as wholes.
Philomela is beautiful, in spite of the obstinate will-
worship of its unrhymed Pindaric : the *Stanzas to
the Memory of Edward Quillinan* are really pathetic,
though slightly irritating in their "sweet simplicity";
and if *Thekla's Answer* is nothing particular, *The
Neckan* nothing but a weaker doublet of the *Merman*,
A Dream is noteworthy in itself, and as an outlier
of the *Marguerite* group. Then we have three things,
of which the first is, though unequal, great at the
close, while the other two rank with the greatest
things Mr Arnold ever did. These are *The Church
of Brou*, *Requiescat*, and *The Scholar-Gipsy*.

If, as no critic ever can, the critic could thoroughly
discover the secret of the inequality of *The Church*

of Brou, he might, like the famous pedant, " put away "
Mr Arnold " fully conjugated in his desk."   The poem
is in theme and scheme purely Romantic, and " nineteenth century " in its looking back to a simple and
pathetic story of the Middle Age—love, bereavement,
and pious resignation.   It is divided into three parts.
The first, in trochaic ballad metre, telling the story,
is one of the poet's weakest things.   You may oft
see as good in Helen Maria Williams and the Della
Cruscans.   The second, describing the church where
the duke and duchess sleep, in an eight-line stanza
of good fashion, is satisfactory but nothing more.
And then the third, after a manner hardly paralleled
save in Crashaw's *Flaming Heart*, breaks from twaddle
and respectable verse into a rocket-rush of heroic
couplets, scattering star-showers of poetry all over and
round the bewildered reader.   It is artifice rather
than art, perhaps, to lisp and drawl, that, when you
do speak out, your speech may be the more effective.
But hardly anything can make one quarrel with such
a piece of poetry as that beginning—

> " So rest, for ever rest, O princely pair ! "

and ending—

> " The rustle of the eternal rain of Love. "

On the other hand, in *Requiescat* there is not a false
note, unless it be the dubious word " vasty " in the
last line ; and even that may shelter itself under the

royal mantle of Shakespeare. The poet has here achieved what he too often fails in, the triple union of simplicity, pathos, and (in the best sense) elegance. The dangerous repetitions of "roses, roses," "tired, tired," &c., come all right ; and above all he has the flexibility and quiver of metre that he too often lacks. His trisyllabic interspersions — the leap in the vein that makes iambic verse alive and passionate—are as happy as they can be, and the relapse into the uniform dissyllabic gives just the right contrast. He must be ἢ θηρίον ἢ θεὸς—and whichever he be, he is not to be envied—who can read *Requiescat* for the first or the fiftieth time without mist in the eyes and without a catch in the voice.

But the greatest of these—the greatest by far—is *The Scholar-Gipsy*. I have read—and that not once only, nor only in the works of unlettered and negligible persons—expressions of irritation at the local Oxonian colour. This is surely amazing. One may not be an Athenian, and never have been at Athens, yet be able to enjoy the local colour of the *Phædrus*. One may not be an Italian, and never have been in Italy, yet find the *Divina Commedia* made not teasing but infinitely vivid and agreeable by Dante's innumerable references to his country, Florentine and general. That some keener thrill, some nobler gust, may arise in the reading of the poem to those who have actually watched

" The line of festal light in Christ Church Hall "

from above Hinksey, who know the Fyfield elm in
May, and have "trailed their fingers in the stripling
Thames" at Bablockhithe,—may be granted. But in
the name of Bandusia and of Gargarus, what offence
can these things give to any worthy wight who by his
ill luck has not seen them with eyes? The objection
is so apt to suggest a suspicion, as illiberal almost as
itself, that one had better not dwell on it.

Let us hope that there are after all few to whom it
has presented itself—that most, even if they be not sons
by actual matriculation of Oxford, feel that, as of other
"Cities of God," they are citizens of her by spiritual
adoption, and by the welcome accorded in all such cities
to God's children. But if the scholar had been an
alumnus of Timbuctoo, and for Cumnor and Godstow
had been substituted strange places in -wa and -ja, I
cannot think that, even to those who are of Oxford, the
intrinsic greatness of this noble poem would be much
affected, though it might lose a separable charm. For
.t has everything—a sufficient scheme, a definite meaning and purpose, a sustained and adequate command
of poetical presentation, and passages and phrases of
the most exquisite beauty. Although it begins as a
pastoral, the mere traditional and conventional frippery
of that form is by no means so prominent in it as in
the later (and, I think, less consummate) companion and
sequel *Thyrsis*. With hardly an exception, the poet
throughout escapes in his phraseology the two main
dangers which so constantly beset him—too great stiff-

ness and too great simplicity. His "Graian" personi-
fication is not overdone; his landscape is exquisite; the
stately stanza not merely sweeps, but sways and swings,
with as much grace as state. And therefore the Arnoldian "note"—the special form of the *maladie du siècle*
which, as we have seen, this poet chooses to celebrate
—acquires for once the full and due poetic expression
and music, both symphonic and in such special
clangours as the never-to-be-too-often-quoted distich—

> "Still nursing the unconquerable hope,
> Still clutching the inviolable shade"—

which marks the highest point of the composition.

The only part on which there may be some difference
between admirers is the final simile of the Tyrian trader.
This finishes off the piece in nineteen lines, of which
the poet was—and justly—proud, which are quite admirable by themselves, but which cannot perhaps produce any very clear evidences of right to be where they
are. No ingenuity can work out the parallel between
the "uncloudedly joyous" scholar who is bid avoid the
palsied, diseased *enfants du siècle*, and the grave Tyrian
who was indignant at the competition of the merry
Greek, and shook out more sail to seek fresh markets.
It is, once more, simply an instance of Mr Arnold's
fancy for an end-note of relief, of cheer, of pleasant
contrast. On his own most rigid principles, I fear it
would have to go as a mere sewn-on patch of purple:
on mine, I welcome it as one of the most engaging

passages of a poem delightful throughout, and at its very best the equal of anything that was written in its author's lifetime, fertile as that was in poetry.

He himself, though he was but just over thirty when this poem appeared, and though his life was to last for a longer period than had passed since his birth to 1853, was to make few further contributions to poetry itself. The reasons of this comparative sterility are interesting, and not quite so obvious as they may appear. It is true, indeed,—it is an arch-truth which has been too rarely recognised,—that something like complete idleness, or at any rate complete freedom from regular mental occupation, is necessary to the man who is to do poetic work great in quality and in quantity at once. The hardest occupation — and Mr Arnold's, though hard, was not exactly that — will indeed leave a man sufficient time, so far as mere time is concerned, to turn out as much verse as the most fertile of poets has ever produced. But then that will scarcely do. The Muses are feminine—and it has been observed that you cannot make up even to the most amiable and reasonable of that sex for refusing to attend to her at the minute when she wants *you*, by devoting even hours, even days, when you are at leisure for *her*. To put the thing more seriously, though perhaps not more truly, the human brain is not so constituted that you can ride or drive or "train" from school to school, examining as you go, for half-a-dozen or half-a-score hours a-day, or that you can devote the same time to the weariest and dreariest of all businesses,

the reading of hundreds of all but identical answers to
the same stock questions, and yet be fresh and fertile
for imaginative composition.   The nearest contradictory
instances to this proposition are those of Scott and
Southey, and they are, in more ways than one or two,
very damaging instances—exceptions which, in a rather
horrible manner, do prove the rule.   To less harassing,
and especially less peremptory, work than Mr Arnold's,
as well as far more literary in kind, Scott sacrificed the
minor literary graces, Southey immolated the choicer
fruits of genius which he undoubtedly possessed the
power of producing ; and both "died from the top
downward.".

But there was something more than this.   Mr
Arnold's poetic ambition, as we have seen, did not aim
at very long and elaborate works.   His forte was the
occasional piece — which might still suggest itself and
be completed—which, as we shall see, did sometimes
suggest itself and was completed—in the intervals, the
holidays, the relaxations of his task.   And if these lucid
and lucent intervals, though existent, were so rare, their
existence and their rarity together suggest that something more than untoward circumstance is to blame for
the fact that they did not show themselves oftener.   A
full and constant tide of inspiration is imperative ; it
will not be denied ; it may kill the poet if he cannot or
will not give vent to it, but it will not be patient of
repression — quietly content to appear now and then,
even on such occasions as the deaths of a Clough and

a Stanley. Nor is it against charity or liberality, while it is in the highest degree consonant with reason and criticism, to infer that Mr Arnold's poetic vein was not very full-blooded, that it was patient of refusal to indulge it, that his poetry, in nearly the happiest of his master's phrases, was not exactly "inevitable," despite the exquisiteness of its quality on occasion.

It is fortunate for the biographer that this earliest part of Mr Arnold's life is so fertile in poetry, for otherwise, in the dearth of information, it would be a terribly barren subject. The thirty years of life yield us hardly twenty pages of letters, of which the first, with its already cited sketch of Laleham, is perhaps the most interesting. At the Trafalgar Square riots of March 1848 the writer is convinced that "the hour of the hereditary peerage and eldest son-ship and immense properties has struck"; sees "a wave of more than American vulgarity, moral, intellectual, and social, preparing to break over us"; and already holds that strange delusion of his that "the French are the most civilised of European peoples." He develops this on the strength of "the intelligence of their idea-moved classes" in a letter to his sister; meets Emerson in April; goes to a Chartist "convention," and has a pleasant legend for Miss Martineau that the late Lord Houghton "refused to be sworn in as a special constable, that he might be free to assume the post of President of the Republic at a moment's notice." He continues to despair of his country as hopelessly as the Tuxford waiter;[1] finds Bournemouth "a very stupid place" — which is distressing; it is a stupid place enough now, but it was not then: "a great moorland covered with furze and low pine coming down to the sea" could never be that—and meets Miss Brontë, "past thirty and plain, with expressive grey eyes though." The rest we must imagine.

[1] "The Tuxford waiter desponds exactly as you do."—*Sydney Smith to Jeffrey.*

CHAPTER II.

LIFE FROM 1851-62——SECOND SERIES OF *POEMS*——
MEROPE——ON TRANSLATING HOMER.

WE must now return a little and give some account of
Mr Arnold's actual life, from a period somewhat before
that reached at the end of the last chapter. The account need not be long, for the life, as has been said,
was not in the ordinary sense eventful; but it is necessary, and can be in this chapter usefully interspersed
with an account of his work, which, for nine of the
eleven years we shall cover, was, though interesting, of
much less interest than that of those immediately before and those immediately succeeding.

One understands at least part of the reason for the
gradual drying up of his poetic vein from a sentence of
his in a letter of 1858, when he and his wife at last took
a house in Chester Square : " It will be something to
unpack one's portmanteau for the first time since I was
married, nearly seven years ago." " Something," indeed ; and one's only wonder is how he, and still more
Mrs Arnold (especially as they now had three children),

could have endured the other thing so long.   There is
no direct information in the *Letters* as to the reason of
this nomadic existence, the only headquarters of which
appear to have been the residence of Mrs Arnold's
father, the judge, in Eaton Place, with flights to friends'
houses and to lodgings at the places of inspection and
others, especially Dover and Brighton.   And guesswork
is nowhere more unprofitable than in cases where private
matters of income, taste, and other things are concerned.
But it certainly would appear, though I have no positive
information on the subject, that in the early days of
State interference with education " My Lords " managed
matters with an equally sublime disregard of the comfort of their officials and the probable efficiency of the
system.[1]

[1] The mystery is partly explained, in a fashion of no little biographical importance, by the statement in Mr Arnold's first general
report for the year 1852, that his district included Lincoln, Notting-
ham, Derby, Stafford, Salop, Hereford, Worcester, Warwick,
Leicester, Rutland and Northants, Gloucester, Monmouth, *all* South
Wales, most of North Wales, and some schools in the East and
West Ridings.   This apparently impossible range had its monstrosity
reduced by the limitation of his inspectorship to Nonconformist
schools of other denominations than the Roman Catholic, especially
Wesleyan and the then powerful " British " schools.   As the schools
multiplied the district was reduced, and at last he had Westminster
only ; but the exclusion of Anglican and Roman Catholic schools
remained till 1870.   And it is impossible not to connect the somewhat exaggerated place which the Dissenters hold in his social and
political theories (as well as perhaps some of his views about the
" Philistine ") with these associations of his.   We must never forget
that for nearly twenty years Mr Arnold worked in the shadow, not
of Barchester Towers, but of Salem Chapel.

Till I noticed the statement quoted opposite, I was quite unable to construct any reasonable theory from such a passage as that in a letter of December 1852[1] and from others which show us Mr Arnold in Lincolnshire, in Shropshire, and in the eastern counties. Even with the elucidation it seems a shockingly bad system. One doubts whether it be worse for an inspector or for the school inspected by him, that he should have no opportunity for food from breakfast to four o'clock, when he staves off death by inviting disease in the shape of the malefic bun; for him or for certain luckless pupil-teachers that, after dinner, he should be "in for [them] till ten o'clock." With this kind of thing when on duty, and no home when off it, a man must begin to appreciate the Biblical passages about partridges, and the wings of a dove, and so forth, most heartily and vividly long before seven years are out, more particularly if he be a man so much given to domesticity as was Matthew Arnold.

However, it was, no doubt, not so bad as it looks. They say the rack is not, though probably no one would care to try. There were holidays; there was a large circle of hospitable family friends, and strangers were only too anxious to welcome (and perhaps to propitiate) Her Majesty's Inspector. The agreeable anomalies of

---

[1] "I have papers sent me to look over which will give me to the 20th of January in *London* without moving, then for a week to *Huntingdonshire* schools, then for another to London, . . . and then *Birmingham* for a month."

the British legal system (which, let Dickens and other
grumblers say what they like, have made many good
people happy and only a few miserable) allowed Mr
Arnold for many years to act (sometimes while simul-
taneously inspecting) as his father-in-law's Marshal on
circuit, with varied company and scenery, little or nothing to do, a handsome fee for doing it, and no worse
rose-leaf in the bed than heavy dinners and hot port
wine, even this being alleviated by " the perpetual haunch
of venison."

For the rest, there are some pleasing miscellaneous
touches in the letters for these years, and there is a
certain liveliness of phrase in them which disappears
in the later.   It is pleasant to find Mr Arnold on
his first visit to Cambridge (where, like a good Wordsworthian, he wanted above all things to see the statue
of Newton) saying what all of us say, " I feel that
the Middle Ages, and all their poetry and impressive-
ness, are in Oxford and not here."   In one letter—
written to his sister " K " (Mrs Forster) as his critical
letters usually are—we find three noteworthy criticisms
on contemporaries, all tinged with that slight want of
cordial appreciation which characterises his criticism
of this kind throughout (except, perhaps, in the case
of Browning).   The first is on Alexander Smith — it
was the time of the undue ascension of the *Life-
Drama* rocket before its equally undue fall.   " It can
do me no good [an odd phrase] to be irritated with
that young man, who certainly has an extraordinary

faculty, although I think he is a phenomenon of a
very dubious character." The second, harsher but
more definite, is on *Villette*. "Why is *Villette* disagree-
able? Because the writer's mind [it is worth remem-
bering that he had met Charlotte Brontë at Miss Martineau's] contains nothing but hunger, rebellion, and
rage, and therefore that is all she can in fact put into
her book. No fine writing can hide this thoroughly,
and it will be fatal to her in the long-run." The Fates
were kinder : and Miss Brontë's mind did contain something besides these ugly things. But it *was* her special
weakness that her own thoughts and experiences were
insufficiently mingled and tempered by a wider knowledge of life and literature. The third is on *My Novel*,
which he says he has "read with great pleasure, though
Bulwer's nature is by no means a perfect one either,
which makes itself felt in his book ; but his gush, his
better humour, his abundant materials, and his mel-
lowed constructive skill — all these are great things."
One would give many pages of the *Letters* for that naïf
admission that "gush" is "a great thing."

A little later (May 1853), all his spare time is being
spent on a poem, which he thinks by far the best thing
he has yet done, to wit, *Sohrab and Rustum*. And
he "never felt so sure of himself or so really and truly
at ease as to criticism." He stays in barracks at the
depot of the 17th Lancers with a brother-in-law, and
we regret to find that "Death or Glory" manners do
not please him. The instance is a cornet spinning his

rings on the table after dinner. " College does civilise
a boy," he ejaculates, which is true—always providing
that it is a good college. Yet, with that almost unconscious naturalness which is particularly noticeable in
him, he is much dissatisfied with Oxford—thinks it (as
we all do) terribly fallen off since *his* days. Perhaps the
infusion of Dissenters' sons (it is just at the time of the
first Commission in 1854) may brace its flaccid sinews,
though the middle-class, he confesses, is abominably dis-
agreeable. He sees a good deal of this poor middle-
class in his inspecting tours, and decides elsewhere
about the same time that "of all dull, stagnant, un-
edifying *entourages*, that of middle-class Dissent is the
stupidest." It is sad to find that he thinks women
utterly unfit for teachers and lecturers ; but Girton
and Lady Margaret's may take comfort, it is "no
natural incapacity, but the fault of their bringing-up."
With regard to his second series of *Poems* (*v. infra*)
he thinks *Balder* will "consolidate the peculiar sort
of reputation he got by *Sohrab and Rustum ;*" and a
little later, in April 1856, we have his own opinion
of himself as a poet, whose charm is "literalness and
simplicity." Mr Ruskin is also treated—with less appreciation than one could wish.

The second series just mentioned was issued in 1855,
a second edition of the first having been called for the
year before. It contained, like its predecessor, such of
his earlier work as he chose to republish and had not
yet republished, chiefly from the *Empedocles* volume.

But *Empedocles* itself was only represented by some scraps, mainly grouped as *The Harp-Player on Etna*. *Faded Leaves*, grouped with an addition, here appear: *Stagirius* is called *Desire*, and the *Stanzas in Memory of the Author of Obermann* now become *Obermann* simply. Only two absolutely new poems, a longer and a shorter, appear: the first is *Balder Dead*, the second *Separation*, the added number of *Faded Leaves*. This is of no great value. *Balder* is interesting, though not extremely good. Its subject is connected with that of Gray's *Descent of Odin*, but handled much more fully, and in blank-verse narrative instead of ballad form. The story, like most of those in Norse mythology, has great capabilities; but it may be questioned whether the Greek-Miltonic chastened style which the poet affects is well calculated to bring them out. The death of Nanna, and the blind fratricide Hoder, are touchingly done, and Hermod's ride to Hela's realm is stately. But as a whole the thing is rather dim and tame.

Mr Arnold's election to the Professorship of Poetry at Oxford (May 1857) was a really notable event, not merely in his own career, but to some, and no small, extent in the history of English literature during the nineteenth century. The post is of no great value. I remember the late Sir Francis Doyle, who was Commissioner of Customs as well as Professor, saying to me once with a humorous melancholy, "Ah! Eau de Cologne pays *much* better than Poetry!" But its duties are far from heavy,

and can be adjusted pretty much as the holder pleases.
And as a position it is unique. It is, though not of
extreme antiquity, the oldest purely literary Professorship
in the British Isles ; and it remained, till long after Mr
Arnold's time, the only one of the kind in the two great
English Universities. In consequence partly of the
regulation that it can be held for ten years only—
nominally five, with a practically invariable re-election
for another five — there is at least the opportunity,
which, since Mr Arnold's own time, has been generally taken, of maintaining and refreshing the distinction of the occupant of the chair. Before his time
there had been a good many undistinguished professors, but Warton and Keble, in their different ways,
must have adorned even a Chair of Poetry even in
the University of Oxford. Above all, the entire (or
almost entire) freedom of action left to the Professor
should have, and in the case of Keble at least had
already had, the most stimulating effect on minds capable of stimulation. For the Professor of Poetry at
Oxford is neither, like some Professors, bound to the
chariot - wheels of examinations and courses of set
teaching, nor, like others, has he to feel that his
best, his most original, efforts can have no interest,
and hardly any meaning, for all but a small circle of
experts. His field is illimitable ; his expatiation in it
is practically untrammelled. It is open to all ; full of
flowers and fruits that all can enjoy ; and it only depends on his own choice and his own literary and

intellectual powers whether his prelections shall take actual rank as literature with the very best of that other literature, with the whole of which, by custom, as an extension from poetry, he is at liberty to deal. In the first century of the chair the custom of delivering these Prelections in Latin had been a slight hamper— indeed to this day it prevents the admirable work of Keble from being known as it should be known. But this was now removed, and Mr Arnold, whose reputation (it could hardly be called fame as yet) was already great with the knowing ones, had not merely Oxford but the English reading world as audience.

And he had it at a peculiarly important time, to the importance of which he himself, in this very position, was not the least contributor. Although the greatest writers of the second period of the century—Tennyson, Browning, Carlyle, Thackeray—had, in all cases but the last, a long, and in the two first a very long and a wonderfully fruitful career still before them, yet the phase to which they belonged was as a dominant phase at its height, and as a crescent was beginning to give place to another. Within a few years—in most cases within a few months —of Mr Arnold's installation, *The Defence of Guenevere* and FitzGerald's *Omar Khayyam* heralded fresh forms of poetry which have not been superseded yet; *The Origin of Species* and *Essays and Reviews* announced changed attitudes of thought; the death of Macaulay removed the last writer who, modern as he was in some ways, and popular, united popularity with a distinctly eighteenth-century tone and tradition; the death of Leigh Hunt removed the last save Landor (always and in all things an outsider) of the great Romantic generation of the first third of the century; *The Ordeal of Richard Feverel* started a new kind of novel.

The division which Mr Arnold, both by office and taste, was called to lead in this newly levied army, was not far from being the most important of all; and it was certainly that of all which required the most thorough reformation of staff, *morale*,[1] and tactics. The English literary criticism of 1830-1860, speaking in round numbers, is curiously and to this day rather unintelligibly bad. There is, no doubt, no set of matters in which it is less safe to generalise than in matters literary, and this is by no means the only instance in which the seemingly natural anticipation that a period of great criticism will follow a period of great creation is falsified. But it most certainly is falsified here. The criticism of the great Romantic period of 1798-1830 was done for it by itself, and in some cases by its greatest practitioners, not by its immediate successors. The philosophic as well as poetical intuition of Coleridge; the marvellous if capricious sympathy and the more marvellous phrase of Lamb; the massive and masculine if not always quite trustworthy or well-governed intellect of Hazlitt, had left no likes behind. Two survivors of this

[1] There are persons who would spell this *moral;* but I am not writing French, and in English the practice of good writers from Chesterfield downwards is my authority.

great race, Leigh Hunt and De Quincey, were indeed
critics, and no inconsiderable ones ; but the natural force
of both had long been much abated, and both had been
not so much critics as essayists ; the tendency of Hunt
to flowery sentimentality or familiar chat, and that of
De Quincey to incessant divergences of "rigmarole,"
being formidable enemies to real critical competence.
The greatest prosemen—not novelists—of the generation now closing, Carlyle and Macaulay, were indeed
both considerable critics.   But the shadow of death in
the one case, the "shadow of Frederick" in the other,
had cut short their critical careers : and presumptuous
as the statement may seem, it may be questioned whether
either had been a great critic—in criticism pure and
simple—of literature.

What is almost more important is that the *average*
literary criticism of William IV.'s reign and of the
first twenty years of her present Majesty's was exceedingly bad.   At one side, of course, the work of men like
Thackeray, who were men of genius but not critics by
profession, or in some respects by equipment, escapes
this verdict.   At the other were men (very few of them
indeed) like Lockhart, who had admirable critical qualifications, but had allowed certain theories and predilec-
tions to harden and ossify within them, and who in
some cases had not outgrown the rough uncivil ways
of the great revolutionary struggle.   Between these the
average critic, if not quite so ignorant of literature as
a certain proportion of the immensely larger body of

reviewers to-day, was certainly even more blind to its
general principles. Such critical work as that of Phillips,
long a favourite pen on the *Times*, and enjoying (I do not
know with how much justice) the repute of being the
person whom Thackeray's *Thunder and Small Beer* has
gibbeted for ever, excites amazement nowadays at its
bland but evidently sincere ignoring of the very rudi-
ments of criticism. I do not know that even in the most
interesting remains of George Brimley (who, had fate
spared him, might have grown into a great as he already
was a good critic) we may not trace something of the
same hopeless amateurishness, the same uncertainty and
"wobbling" between the expression of unconnected and
unargued likes and dislikes concerning the matter of the
piece, and real critical considerations on its merits or
demerits of scheme and form.

Not for the first time help came to us Trojans *Graia
ab urbe.* Of the general merits of French literary criticism it is possible to entertain a somewhat lower idea
than that which (in consequence of the very circumstances with which we are now dealing) it has been
for many years fashionable in England to hold. But
between 1830 and 1860 the French had a very strong
critical school indeed — a school whose scholars and
masters showed the dæmonic, or at least prophetic,
inspiration of Michelet, the milder and feebler but still
inspiring enthusiasm of Quinet, the academic clearness
and discipline of Villemain and Nisard, the Lucianic
wit of Mérimée, the matchless appreciation of Gautier,

and, above all, the great new critical idiosyncrasy of Sainte-Beuve. Between these men there were the widest possible differences, not merely of personal taste and genius, but of literary theory and practice. But where they all differed quite infinitely from the lower class of English critics, and favourably from all but the highest in their happiest moments, was in a singular mixture of scholarship and appreciation. Even the most Romantic of them usually tried to compare the subject with its likes in his own and even, to some extent, in other literatures; even the most Classical acknowledged, to some extent, that it was his duty to appreciate, to understand, to grasp the case of the victim before ordering him off to execution.

In the practice of Sainte-Beuve himself, these two acknowledgments of the duty of the critic embraced each other in the happiest union. The want of enthusiasm which has been sometimes rather sillily charged against him, comes in reality to no more than this —that he is too busy in analysing, putting together again, comparing, setting things in different lights and in different companies, to have much time for dithyrambs. And the preference of second- to first-class subjects, which has been also urged, is little more than the result of the fact that these processes are more telling, more interesting, and more needed in the case of the former than in the case of the latter. Homer, Æschylus, Lucretius, Dante, Shakespeare will always make their own way with all fit readers sooner or later: it is not so

with Meleager or Macrobius or Marmontel, with William
Langland or with Thomas Love Peacock.

But Sainte-Beuve must not carry us too far from Mr
Arnold, all important as was the influence of the one
upon the other.   It is enough to say that the new Professor of Poetry (who might be less appetisingly but
more correctly called a Professor of Criticism) had long
entertained the wish to attempt, and now had the means
of effecting, a reform in English criticism, partly on
Sainte-Beuve's own lines, partly on others which he had
already made publicly known in his famous Preface, and
in some later critical writings, and which he was for the
rest of his life always unflinchingly to champion, sometimes rather disastrously to extend.

Still it has always been held that this chair is not
merely a chair of criticism ; and Mr Arnold lodged a
poetical diploma-piece in the shape of *Merope*.   This
was avowedly written as a sort of professorial manifesto
—a document to show what the only Professor of
Poetry whom England allowed herself thought, in theory
and practice, of at least dramatic poetry.   It was, as
was to be expected from the author's official position
and his not widespread but well-grounded reputation,
much less neglected than his earlier poetry had been.
He even tells us that "it sells well" ; but the reviewers
were not pleased.   The *Athenæum* review is "a choice
specimen of style," and the *Spectator* "of argumentation";
the *Saturday Review* is only "deadly prosy," but none
were exactly favourable till G. H. Lewes in *The Leader*

was "very gratifying." Private criticism was a little kinder. The present Archbishop of Canterbury (to whom, indeed, Mr Arnold had just given "a flaming testimonial for Rugby") read it "with astonishment at its goodness," a sentence which, it may be observed, is a little double-edged. Kingsley (whom the editor of the *Letters* good-naturedly but perhaps rather superfluously reintroduces to the British public as "author of *The Saints' Tragedy* and other poems") was "very handsome." Froude, though he begs the poet to "discontinue the line," was not uncomplimentary in other ways. His own conclusion, from reviews and letters together, is pretty plainly put in two sentences, that he "saw the book was not going to take as he wished," and that "she [Merope] is more calculated to inaugurate my professorship with dignity than to move deeply the present race of *humans*." Let us see what "she" is actually like.

It is rather curious that the story of Merope should have been so tempting as, to mention nothing else, Maffei's attempt in Italian, Voltaire's in French, and this of Mr Arnold's in English, show it to have been to modern admirers and would-be practitioners of the Classical drama : and the curiosity is of a tell-tale kind. For the fact is that the *donnée* is very much more of the Romantic than of the Classical description, and offers much greater conveniences to the Romantic than to the Classical practitioner. With minor variations, the story as generally dramatised is this. Merope, the widowed queen of the murdered Heraclid Cresphontes, has saved her youngest son from the murderer and usurper, Polyphontes, and sent him out of the country. When he has grown up, and has secretly returned to Messenia to take vengeance, Polyphontes is pressing Merope to let bygones be bygones and marry him, so as to reconcile the jarring parties in the State. Æpytus, the son, to facilitate his reception, represents himself as a messenger charged to bring the news of his own death ; and Merope, hearing this and believing the messenger to be also the assassin, obtains access to the chamber where he is resting after his journey, and is about to murder her own sleeping son when he is saved by the inevitable *anagnorisis.* The party of Cresphontes is then secretly roused. Æpytus, at the sacrifice which the tyrant holds in honour of the news of his rival's death, snatches the sacrificial axe and kills Polyphontes himself, and all ends well.

There is, of course, a strong dramatic moment here ; but I cannot think the plot by any means an ideal one for classical tragedy. At any rate the Aristotelian conditions—the real ones, not the fanciful distortions of sixteenth-seventeenth century criticism—are very ill satisfied. There is bloodshed, but there is no tragic bloodshed, as there would have been had Merope actually killed her son. The arresting and triumphant "grip" of the tragic misfortunes of Œdipus and Orestes, the combination of the course of fate and the ἁμαρτία of the individual, is totally absent. The wooing of Merope

by Polyphontes is not so much preposterous as insignificant, though Voltaire, by a touch of modernism, has
rescued it or half-rescued it from this most terrible of
limbos. The right triumphs, no doubt ; but who cares
whether it does or not ? And Mr Arnold, with the
heroic obstinacy of the doctrinaire, has done nothing to
help the effect of a scheme in itself sufficiently uninspir-
ing to the modern reader. When he was at work upon
the piece he had " thought and hoped " that it would
have what Buddha called " the character of Fixity, that
true sign of the law." A not unfriendly critic might
have pointed out, with gloomy forebodings, that a sign
of law is not necessarily a sign of poetry, and that, as
a prophet of his own had laid it down, poetry should
" transport " not " fix." At any rate, it is clear to any
one who reads the book that the author was in a mood
of deliberate provocation and exaggeration — not a
favourable mood for art. The quiet grace of Sophocles
is perhaps impossible to reproduce in English, but Mr
Arnold's verse is more than quiet, it is positively tame.
The dreary *tirades* of Polyphontes and Merope, and
their snip-snap *stichomythia*, read equally ill in English.
Mr Swinburne, who has succeeded where Mr Arnold
failed, saw by a true intuition that, to equal the effect
of the Greek chorus, full English lyric with rhyme and
musical sweep was required. Mr Arnold himself, as
might have been expected from his previous experiments in unrhymed Pindarics, has given us strophes and
antistrophes most punctiliously equivalent in syllables ;

but sometimes with hardly any, and never with very much, vesture of poetry about them. It is absolutely preposterous to suppose that the effect on a Greek ear of a strophe even of Sophocles or Euripides, let alone the great Agamemnonian choruses, was anything like the effect on an English ear of such wooden stuff as this :—

> " Three brothers roved the field,
> And to two did Destiny
> Give the thrones that they conquer'd,
> But the third, what delays him
> From his unattained crown ? "

But Mr Arnold would say " This is your unchaste modern love for passages and patches. Tell me how I managed this worthy action?" To which the only answer can be, "Sir, the action is rather uninteresting. Save at one moment you have not raised the interest anywhere, and you have certainly not made the most of it there."

The fact is, that very few even of thorough-going Arnoldians have had, or, except merely as "fighting a prize," could have had, much to say for *Merope*. The author pleads that he only meant "to give people a specimen of the world created by the Greek imagination." In the first place, one really cannot help (with the opening speech of the *Prometheus*, and the close of the *Eumenides*, and the whole of the *Agamemnon* in one's mind) saying that this is rather hard on the Greeks. And in the second place, what a curious way of setting about the object, when luckily specimens of the actual

"world" so "created," not mere *pastiches* and plaster
models of them, are still to be had, and of the very
best! But the fact is, thirdly, that Mr Arnold, as all
men so often do, and as he not very seldom did, was
clearly trying not so much to extol one thing as to
depreciate another. Probably in his heart of hearts
(which is generally a much wiser heart than that according to which the mouth speaks and the pen writes) he
knew his failure. At any rate, he never attempted anything of the kind again, and Merope, that queen of
plaster, remains alone in his gallery, with, as we see
in other galleries, merely some *disjecta membra*—"Fragment of an *Antigone*," "Fragment of a *Dejaneira*,"
grouped at her feet. In the definitive edition indeed, she is not with these but with *Empedocles on
Etna*, a rather unlucky contrast. For *Empedocles*, if
very much less deliberately Greek than *Merope*, is very
much better poetry, and it is almost impossible that the
comparison of the two should not suggest to the reader
that the attempt to be Greek is exactly and precisely
the cause of the failure to be poetical. Mr Arnold had
forgotten his master's words about the *oikeia hedone*.
The pleasure of Greek art is one thing—the pleasure
of English poetry another.

His inaugural lecture, "On the Modern Element
in Literature," was printed many years afterwards in
Macmillan's Magazine for February 1869; and this
long hesitation seems to have been followed by an
even longer repentance, for the piece was never in-

cluded in any one of his volumes of essays. But the ten years of his professorship are, according to the wise parsimony of the chair, amply represented by the two famous little books — *On Translating Homer*, which, with its supplementary "Last Words," appeared in 1861 - 62, and *On the Study of Celtic Literature*, which appeared at the termination of his tenure in 1867. It may be questioned whether he ever did anything of more influence than these books, this being due partly to the fashion of their publication — which, in the latter case at least, applied the triple shock of lecture at the greatest of English literary centres, of magazine article, and of book — and partly to the fact that they were about subjects in which a real or a factitious, a direct or an indirect, interest was taken by almost every one. Every educated person knew and cared something (or at least would not have liked to be supposed not to care and know something) about Homer ; very few educated persons knew anything about Celtic literature. But in these later lectures he put in a more popular and provocative form than that of his *French Eton* (see next chapter) that mixture of literary, political, social, and miscellaneous critique of his countrymen for which he was thenceforward best known ; and which, if it brought down some hard knocks from his adversaries, and perhaps was not altogether a healthy mixture for himself, could at least not be charged by any reasonable person with lack of piquancy and actuality.

Both books are, and, and, despite some drawbacks of personal and ephemeral allusion, always will be, interesting; and both had, perhaps even more than the *Essays in Criticism* themselves, a stimulating effect upon English men of letters which can hardly be overvalued. It may indeed be said without paradox that they owe not a little of their value to their faults; but they owe a great deal more to their merits.

The faults are apparent enough even in the first series, which falls to be noticed in this chapter; yet it is really difficult to say when a more important book of English criticism had appeared. Dryden's *Essay of Dramatic Poesy*, Johnson's *Lives* at their frequent best, Coleridge's *Biographia Literaria*, are greater things; but hardly the best of them was in its day more " important for *us*." To read even the best of that immediately preceding criticism of which something has been said above — nay, even to recur to Coleridge and Hazlitt and Lamb — and then to take up *On Translating Homer*, is to pass to a critic with a far fuller equipment, with a new method, with a style of his own, and with an almost entirely novel conception of the whole art of criticism. For the first time (even Coleridge with much wider reading had not co-ordinated it from this point of view) we find the two great ancient and the three or four great modern literatures of Europe taken synoptically, used to illustrate and explain each other, to point out each other's defects and throw up each other's merits.

Almost for the first time, too, we have ancient literature treated more or less like modern — neither from
the merely philological point of view, nor with reference to the stock platitudes and traditions about it.
The critic is not afraid of doctrines and general
principles—in fact, he is rather too fond of them—
but his object is anything rather than mere arid
deduction and codification. He has the æsthetic
sense as thoroughly as Hazlitt and Lamb, but without
the wilfulness of either, or at least with a different
kind of wilfulness from that of either. Finally, in
one of the numerous ways in which he shows that
his subject is alive to him, he mixes it up with the
queerest personalities and sudden zigzags, with all
manner of digressions and side‑flings. And last of
all, he has that new style of which we spoke—a style
by no means devoid of affectation and even trick,
threatening, to experienced eyes, the disease of mannerism, but attractive in its very provocations, almost
wholly original, and calculated, at least while it retains
its freshness, to drive what is said home into the
reader's mind and to stick it there.

The faults, we said, both critical and non‑critical,
are certainly not lacking ; and if they were not partly
excused by the author's avowedly militant position,
might seem sometimes rather grave. Whatever may
have been the want of taste, and even the want of
sense, in the translation of F. W. Newman, it is almost
sufficient to say that they were neither greater nor

less than might have been expected from a person
who, if the most scholarly of eccentrics, was also the
most eccentric even of English scholars. It is difficult not to think that Mr Arnold makes too much
of them and refers too frequently to them. Such
"iteration" is literally "damnable": it must be con-
demned as unfair, out of place, out of taste, and even
not distantly approaching that lack of urbanity with
which Mr Arnold was never tired of reproaching his
countrymen. Another translator, Mr Wright, was indeed needlessly sensitive to Mr Arnold's strictures;
but these strictures themselves were needlessly severe.
It is all very well for a reviewer, especially if he be
young and anonymous, to tell a living writer that his
book has "no reason for existing"; but chairs of
literature are not maintained by universities that their
occupants may, in relation to living persons, exercise
the functions of young anonymous reviewers. It may
indeed be doubted whether these occupants should,
except in the most guarded way, touch living persons
at all.

Critically too, as well as from the point of view of
manners, the *Lectures on Translating Homer* are open
to not a few criticisms. In the first place, the assumptions are enormous, and, in some cases at least,
demonstrably baseless. One of Mr Arnold's strongest
points, for instance, not merely against Mr Newman
but against Homeric translators generally, is concerned
with the renderings of the Homeric compound adjec-

tives, especially the stock ones—*koruthaiolos, merops*, and the rest. The originals, he is never weary of repeating, did not strike a Greek and do not strike a Greek scholar as out of the way ; the English equivalents do so strike an English reader. Now as to the Greeks themselves, we know nothing : they have left us no positive information on the subject. But if (which is no doubt at least partly true) *koruthaiolos* and *dolichoskion* do not strike us, who have been familiar with Greek almost as long as we can remember, as out of the way, is that an argument? Most of us, I suppose, at about nine or ten years old, some no doubt a little or a good deal earlier, learnt these words as part of the ordinary Greek that was presented to us, just as much as *kai* and *ara ;* but if we had learnt Greek as we learn English, beginning with quite ordinary words, would it be so? I think not; nor would it be so if people began Greek at a later and more critical stage of their education.

It is also true that the book is full of that exceedingly arbitrary and unproved assertion, of that rather fanciful terminology, of those sometimes questionable æsthetic *obiter dicta*, of which, from first to last, Mr Arnold was so prolific. When he talks about the mysterious "grand style," and tells us that Milton can never be affected, we murmur, "*De gustibus !*" and add mentally, "Though Milton is the greatest of affected writers, Milton is, after *Comus* at least, never anything else !" When he tells us again that at that moment (1861) "English literature as a living intellectual instrument ranks after the literatures of France and Germany," we remember that at the time France possessed perhaps only one writer, Victor Hugo, and Germany absolutely none, of the calibre of a dozen Englishmen — Tennyson, Browning, Carlyle, Thackeray, Dickens, and not a few others, from Landor to Mr Ruskin ; that Germany, further, had scarcely one, though France had more than one or two, great writers of the second class : and we say, "Either your 'living intellectual instrument' is a juggle of words, or you really are neglecting fact." Many— very many—similar retorts are possible ; and the most hopeless variance of all must come when we arrive at Mr Arnold's championship of that ungainly and sterile mule the English hexameter, and when we review the specimens of the animal that he turns out from his own stables for our inspection.

But it matters not. For all this, and very much more than all this, which may be passed over as unnecessary or improper, nothing like the book had, for positive critical quality, and still more for germinal influence, been seen by its generation, and nothing of the same quality and influence has been seen for more than a technical generation since. It would of course be uncritical in the last degree to take the change in English criticism which followed as wholly and directly Mr Arnold's work. He was not even the voice crying in the wilderness : only one of many voices in a land ready at least to be eared and pathed. But he was the earliest of such voices, the clearest, most original, most potent ; and a great deal of what followed was directly due to him.

The non-literary events of his life during this period were sufficiently varied if not very momentous. We have mentioned the domiciling in Chester Square, which took place in February 1858, perhaps on the strength of the additional income from Oxford. In the late summer of that year he went alone to Switzerland, and next spring, shortly after the New Year, received, to his very great joy, a roving commission to France, Belgium, Switzerland, and Piedmont, to report on elementary education. " Foreign life," he says, with that perfect naturalness which makes the charm of his letters, " is still to me perfectly delightful and liberating in the last degree." And he was duly " presented " at home, in order that he might be presentable abroad. But the first days of the actual sojourn (as we have them recorded in a letter to his mother of April 14) were saddened by that death of his brother William, which he has enshrined in verse.

He had, however, plenty to distract him. France was all astir with the Austrian war, and it is impossible to read his expressions of half-awed admiration of French military and other greatness without rather mischievous amusement. He visited the Morbihan, which struck him as it must strike every one. Here

he is pathetic over a promising but not performing
dinner at Auray — " soup, Carnac oysters, shrimps,
fricandeau of veal, breast of veal, and asparagus ; " but
" everything so detestable" that his dinner was bread
and cheese. He must have been unlucky : the little
Breton inns, at any rate a few years later than this,
used, it is true, to be dirty to an extent appalling to
an Englishman ; but their provender was usually far
from contemptible. There is more sense of Breton
scenery in another letter a little later. Both here
and, presently, in Gascony he notes truly enough
" the incredible degree to which the Revolution has
cleared the feudal ages out of the minds of the country
people" ; but if he reflected on the bad national effect
of this breach with the past, he does not say so.
By June 12 he is in Holland, and does not like it
— weather, language, &c., all English in the worst
sense, apparently without the Norman and Latin element which just saves us. And though he was a
very short time in the Netherlands, he has to relieve
his feelings by more abuse of them when he gets
back to Paris—in fact, he speaks of Holland exactly
as the typical Frenchman speaks of England, and is
accordingly very funny to read. The two things that
make Holland most interesting, history and art, were
exactly those that appealed to Mr Arnold least. Then
after a refreshing bath of Paris, he goes to Strasbourg,
and Time—Time the Humourist as well as the Avenger
and Consoler—makes him commit himself dreadfully.

He "thinks there cannot be a moment's doubt" that the French will beat the Prussians even far more completely and rapidly than they are beating the Austrians. Lord Cowley, it seems, "entirely shared" his conviction that "the French will always beat any number of Germans who come into the field against them, and never be beaten by any one but the English." Let us hope that Jove, when he whistled half this prophecy down the wind, affirmed the rest of it! Switzerland comes next; and he is beginning to want very much to be back in England, partly "for the children, but partly also from affection for that foolish old country"—which paternal and patriotic desire was granted about the end of the month, though only for a short time, during which he wrote a pamphlet on the Italian question. Then "M. le Professeur Docteur Arnold, Directeur Général de toutes les Écoles de la Grande Bretagne," returned to France for a time, saw Mérimée and George Sand and Renan, as well as a good deal of Sainte-Beuve, and was back again for good in the foolish old country at the end of the month.

In the early winter of 1859-60 we find him a volunteer, commenting not too happily on "the hideous English toadyism which invests lords and great people with commands," a remark which seems to clench the inference that he had not appreciated the effect of the Revolution upon France. For nearly three parts of 1860 we have not a single letter, except one in January pleasantly referring to his youngest child "in black velvet and red-and-white tartan, looking such a duck that it was hard to take one's eyes off him." [1] This letter, by the way, ends with an odd admission from the author of the remark quoted just now. He says of the Americans, "It seems as if few stocks could be trusted to grow up properly without having a priesthood and an aristocracy to act as their schoolmasters at some time or other of their national existence." This is a confession. The gap, however, is partly atoned for by a very pleasant batch in September from Viel Salm in the Ardennes, where the whole family spent a short time, and where the Director-General of all the schools in Great Britain had splendid fishing, the hapless Ardennes trout being only accustomed to nets.

Then the interest returns to literature, and the lectures on translating Homer, and Tennyson's "deficiency in intellectual power," and Mr Arnold's own interest in the Middle Ages, which may surprise some folk. It seems that he has "a strong sense of the irrationality of that period" and of "the utter folly of those who take it seriously and play at restoring it." Still it has "poetically the greatest charm and refreshment for me." One may perhaps be permitted to doubt whether you can get much real poetical refreshment out of a thing which is irrational

[1] The letters are full of pleasant child-worship, the best passage of all being perhaps the dialogue between Tom and "Budge," at vol. i. p. 56, with the five-year-old cynicism of the elder's reply, "Oh this is *false* Budge, this is all *false!*" to his infant brother's protestations of affection.

and which you don't take seriously : the practice seems
to be not unlike that mediæval one of keeping fools for
your delectation. Nor can the observations on Tennyson be said to be quite just or quite pleasant. But every
age and every individual is unjust to his or its immediate
predecessor—a saying dangerous and double-edged, but
true for all that. Then he "entangles himself in the
study of accents"—it would be difficult to find any ad-
venturer who has *not* entangled himself in that study—
and groans over "a frightful parcel of grammar papers,"
which he only just "manages in time," apparently on the
very unwholesome principle (though this was not the
same batch) of doing twenty before going to bed when
he comes in from a dinner-party at eleven o'clock.
Colds, Brighton, praise from Sainte-Beuve, critical attacks
in the English papers, and (not quite unprovoked) from
F. W. Newman, reflections on the Age of Wisdom (forty),
and a meeting with Thackeray, the Laureate of that age,
diversify the history agreeably. Then we come to a
dead, and now rather more than dull, controversy over
the Revised Code, of which we need not say much.
Official etiquette on such matters, especially in England,
is very loose, though he himself seems to have at one
time thought it distantly possible, though not likely, that
he would be ejected for the part he took. And his first
five years' tenure of the Oxford Chair ends with the
delivery of the Creweian oration, as to the composition
of which he consoles himself (having heard both from
the Vice-Chancellor and others that there was to be "a

great row ") by reflecting that "it doesn't much matter what he writes, as he shall not be heard." I do not know whether the prediction was justified; but if so, the same fate had, according to tradition, befallen his New-digate some twenty years earlier. In neither case can the "row" have had any personal reference. Though his lectures were never largely attended by undergraduates, he was always popular in Oxford.

CHAPTER III.

THE period of Mr Arnold's second tenure of the Poetry
Chair, from 1862 to 1867, was much more fertile in remarkable books than that of his first. It was during
this time that he established himself at once as the leader
of English critics by his *Essays in Criticism* (some of
which had first taken form as Oxford Lectures) and that
he made his last appearance with a considerable collection of *New Poems.* It was during this, or immediately
after its expiration, that he issued his second collected
book of lectures on *The Study of Celtic Literature ;* and
it was then that he put in more popular, though still in
not extremely popular, forms the results of his investi-
gations into Continental education. It was during this
time also that his thoughts took the somewhat unfortunate twist towards the mission of reforming his country, not merely in matters literary, where he was excellently qualified for the apostolate, but in the much more

dubiously warranted function of political, "sociological," and above all, ecclesiastical or anti-ecclesiastical gospeller. With all these things we must now deal.

No one of Mr Arnold's books is more important, or more useful in studying the evolution of his thought and style, than *A French Eton* (1864). Although he was advancing in middle-life when it was written, and had evidently, as the phrase goes, "made up his bundle of prejudices," he had not written, or at least published, very much prose; his mannerisms had not hardened. And above all, he was but just catching the public ear, and so was not tempted to assume the part of Chester-field-Socrates, which he played later, to the diversion of some, to the real improvement of many, but a little to his own disaster. He was very thoroughly acquainted with the facts of his subject, which was not always the case later; and though his assumptions—the insensibility of aristocracies to ideas, the superiority of the French to the English in this respect, the failure of the Anglican Church, and so forth—are already as questionable as they are confident, he puts them with a certain modesty, a certain ἐπιείκεια, which was perhaps not always so obvious when he came to preach that quality itself later. About the gist of the book it is not necessary to say very much. He practically admits the obvious and unanswerable objection that his *French Eton*, whether we look for it at Toulouse or look for it at Sorèze, is very French, but not at all Eton. He does not really attempt to meet the more dangerous though

less epigrammatic demurrer, " Do you *want* schools to
turn out products of this sort ? "   It was only indirectly
his fault, but it was a more or less direct consequence of
his arguments, that a process of making ducks and drakes
of English grammar-school endowments began, and was
(chiefly in the " seventies ") carried on, with results, the
mischievousness of which apparently has been known
and noted only by experts, and which they have chiefly
kept to themselves.

All this is already ancient history, and history not
ancient enough to be venerable.   But the book as a
book, and also as a document in the case, has, and
always will have, interest.   " The cries and catch-
words " which Mr Arnold denounces, as men so often
do denounce their own most besetting temptations,
have not yet quite mastered him ; but they have made
a lodgment.   The revolt—in itself quite justifiable, and
even admirable — from the complacent acceptance of
English middle-class thought, English post-Reform-Bill
politics, English mid-century taste and ethics and philosophy,—from everything, in short, of which Macaulay
was the equally accepted and representative eulogist
and exponent, is conspicuous.   It is from foreign and
almost hostile sources that we must expect help.   The
State is to resume, or to initiate, its guidance of a very
large part, if not of the whole, of the matters which
popular thought, Liberal and Conservative alike, then
assigned to individual action or private combination.
We have not yet Barbarians, Philistines, and Populace

labelled with their tickets and furnished with their
descriptions ; but the three classes are already sharply
separated in Mr Arnold's mind, and we can see that
only in the Philistine who burns Dagon, and accepts cir-
cumcision and culture fully, is there to be any salvation.
The anti-clerical and anti-theological animus is already
strong ; the attitude *dantis jura Catonis* is arranged ; the
jura themselves, if not actually graven and tabulated,
can be seen coming with very little difficulty. Above
all, the singing-robes are pretty clearly laid aside ; the
Scholar-Gipsy exercises no further spell ; we have turned
to prose and (as we can best manage it) sense.

But *A French Eton* is perhaps most interesting for its
style. In this respect it marks a stage, and a distinct
one, between the *Preface* of 1853 and the later and
better known works. More of a *concio ad vulgus* than
the former, it shows a pretty obvious endeavour to
soften and popularise, without unduly vulgarising, the
academic tone of the earlier work. And it does not
yet display those "mincing graces" which were sometimes attributed (according to a very friendly and most
competent critic, "harshly, but justly") to the later.
The mannerisms, indeed, like the dogmatisms, are
pretty clearly imminent. Slightly exotic vocabulary—
"habitude," "repartition," for "habit," "distribution"
—makes its appearance. That abhorrence of the con-
junqtion, which made Mr Arnold later give us rows of
adjectives and substantives, with never an "and" to
string them together, is here. But no one of these

tricks, nor any other, is present in excess : there is
nothing that can justly be called falsetto ; and in es-
pecial, though some names of merely ephemeral interest are in evidence — Baines, Roebuck, Miall, &c.,
Mr Arnold's well - known substitutes for Cleon and
Cinesias—there is nothing like the torrent of personal
allusion in *Friendship's Garland.* " Bottles " and his
company are not yet with us ; the dose of *persiflage*
is rigorously kept down ; the author has not reached the
stage when he seemed to hold sincerely the principle so
wickedly put by Mr Lewis Carroll, that

" What I tell you three times is true,"

and that the truth could be made truest by making the
three thirty.

The result is that he never wrote better. A little
of the dignity of his earlier manner—when he simply
followed that admirable older Oxford style, of which
Newman was the greatest master and the last — is
gone, but it has taken some stiffness with it. Some
—indeed a good deal—of the piquancy of the later
is not yet apparent ; but its absence implies, and is
more than compensated by, the concomitant absence
of those airs and flings, those interludes as of an academic jester, in cap and gown and liripipe instead of
motley, which have been charged, not quite unjustly, on
the Arnold that we know best. There is hardly in
English a better example of the blending and concilia-
tion of the two modes of argumentative writing referred

to in Bishop Hurd's acute observation, that if your first object is to convince, you cannot use a style too soft and insinuating ; if you want to confute, the rougher and more unsparing the better. And the description and characterisation are quite excellent.

Between *A French Eton* and the second collection of Oxford Lectures came, in 1865, the famous *Essays in Criticism*, the first full and varied, and perhaps always the best, expression and illustration of the author's critical attitude, the detailed manifesto and exemplar of the new critical method, and so one of the epoch-making books of the later nineteenth century in English. It consisted, in the first edition, of a *Preface* (afterwards somewhat altered and toned down) and of nine essays (afterwards to be made ten by the addition of *A Persian Passion-Play*). The two first of these were general, on *The Function of Criticism at the Present Time* and *The Literary Influence of Academies*, while the other seven dealt respectively with the two Guérins, Heine, *Pagan and Mediæval Religious Sentiment*, Joubert, Spinoza, and Marcus Aurelius. I am afraid it must be taken as only too strong a confirmation of Mr Arnold's own belief as to the indifference of the English people to criticism that no second edition of this book was called for till four years were past, no third for ten, and no fourth for nearly twenty.

Yet, to any one whom the gods have made in the very slightest degree critical, it is one of the most

fascinating (if sometimes also one of the most pro-
voking) of books; and the fascination and provocation should surely have been felt even by others. As
always with the author, there is nothing easier than
to pick holes in it: in fact, on his own principles,
one is simply bound to pick holes. He evidently
enjoyed himself very much in the *Preface:* but it
may be doubted whether the severe Goddess of Taste
can have altogether smiled on his enjoyment. He
is superciliously bland to the unlucky and no doubt
rather unwise Mr Wright (*v. supra*): he tells the
Guardian in a periphrasis that it is dull, and "Pres-
byter Anglicanus" that he is born of Hyrcanian
tigers, and the editor of the *Saturday Review* that
he is a late and embarrassed convert to the Philistines. He introduces not merely Mr Spurgeon, a
Philistine of some substance and memory, but hapless forgotten shadows like "Mr Clay," "Mr Dif-
fanger," "Inspector Tanner," "Professor Pepper" to
the contempt of the world. And then, when we are
beginning to find all this laughter rather "thorn-
crackling" and a little forced, the thing ends with
the famous and magnificent *epiphonema* (as they would
have said in the old days) to Oxford, which must for ever
conciliate all sons of hers and all gracious outsiders
to its author, just as it turns generation after generation of her enemies sick with an agonised grin.

So, again, one may marvel, and almost grow angry,
at the whim which made Mr Arnold waste two whole

essays on an amiable and interesting person like
Eugénie de Guérin and a mere nobody like her
brother. They are very pretty essays in themselves;
but then (as Mr Arnold has taught us), "all depends
on the subject," and the subjects here are so exceedingly unimportant! Besides, as he himself almost
openly confessed, and as everybody admits now, he
really did not understand French poetry at all. When
we come to "Keats and Guérin," there is nothing for
it but to take refuge in Byron's

> "*Such* names coupled !"

and pass with averted face. Seventy-two mortal pages
of Matthew Arnold's, at his very best time, wasted on
a brother and sister who happened to be taken up by
Sainte-Beuve !

But the rest of the book is entirely free from liability
to any such criticism as this. To some criticism—even
to a good deal—it is beyond doubt exposed. The first
and most famous paper—the general manifesto, as the
earlier *Preface* to the *Poems* is the special one, of its
author's literary creed—on *The Function of Criticism at
the Present Time* must indeed underlie much the same
objections as those that have been made to the introduction. Here is the celebrated passage about "Wragg is
in custody," the text of which, though no doubt painful in subject and inurbane in phraseology, is really
a rather slender basis on which to draw up an in-
dictment against a nation. Here is the astounding—

the, if serious, almost preternatural — statement that "not very much of current English literature comes into this best that is known and thought in the world. Not very much I fear : certainly less than of the current literature of France and Germany." And this was 1865, when the Germans had had no great poet but Heine for a generation, nor any great poets but Goethe and Heine for some five hundred years, no great prose-writer but Heine (unless you call Goethe one), and were not going to have any! It was 1865, when all the great French writers, themselves of but some thirty years' standing, were dying off, not to be succeeded! 1865, when for seventy years England had not lacked, and for nearly thirty more was not to lack, poets and prose-writers of the first order by the dozen and almost the score! Here, too, is the marvellous companion-statement that in the England of the first quarter of the century was "no national glow of life." It was the chill of death, I suppose, which made the nation fasten on the throat of the world and choke it into submission during a twenty years' struggle.

But these things are only Mr Arnold's way. I have never been able to satisfy myself whether they were deliberate paradoxes, or sincere and rather pathetic paralogisms. For instance, did he really think that the *Revue des Deux Mondes*, an organ of "dukes, dunces, and *dévotes*," as it used to be called even in those days by the wicked knowing ones, a nursing mother of Academies certainly, and a most respectable periodical in all ways — that this good *Revue* actually "had for its main function to understand and utter the best that is known and thought in the world," absolutely existed as an organ for "the free play of mind"? I should be disposed to think that the truer explanation of such things is that they were neither quite paradoxes nor quite paralogisms; but the offspring of an innocent willingness to believe what he wished, and of an almost equally innocent desire to provoke the adversary. Unless (as unluckily they sometimes are) they be taken at the foot of the letter, they can do no harm, and their very piquancy helps the rest to do a great deal of good.

For there can be no doubt that in the main contention of his manifesto, as of his book, Mr Arnold was absolutely right. It was true that England, save for spasmodic and very partial appearances of it in a few of her great men of letters—Ben Jonson, Dryden, Addison, Johnson—had been wonderfully deficient in criticism up to the end of the eighteenth century; and that though in the early nineteenth she had produced one great philosophical critic, another even greater on the purely literary side, and a third of unique appreciative sympathy, in Coleridge, Hazlitt, and Lamb, she had not followed these up, and had, even in them, shown certain critical limitations. It was true that though the Germans had little and the French nothing to teach us in range, both had much to teach us in thoroughness, method, *style* of criticism. And it was truest of all (though Mr Arnold, who did not like the historic estimate, would have admitted this with a certain grudge) that the time imperatively demanded a thorough "stock - taking" of our own literature in the light and with the help of others.

Let the *palma*—let the *maxima palma*—of criticism be given to him in that he first fought for the creed of this literary orthodoxy, and first exemplified (with whatever admixture of will-worship of his own, with whatever quaint rites and ceremonies) the carrying out of the cult. It is possible that his direct influence may have been exaggerated ; one of the most necessary, though not of the most grateful, businesses of the literary historian is to point out that with rare exceptions, and those almost wholly on the poetic side, great men of letters rather show in a general, early, and original fashion a common tendency than definitely lead an otherwise sluggish multitude to the promised land. But no investigation has deprived, or is at all likely to deprive, the *Essays in Criticism* of their place as an epoch-making book, as the manual of a new and often independent, but, on the whole, like-minded, critical movement in England.

Nor can the blow of the first essay be said to be ill followed up in the second, the almost equally famous (perhaps the *more* famous) *Influence of Academies*. Of course here also, here as always, you may make reservations. It is a very strong argument, an argument stronger than any of Mr Arnold's, that the institutions of a nation, if they are to last, if they are to do any good, must be in accordance with the spirit of the nation; that if the French Academy has been beneficial, it is because the French spirit is academic; and that if (as we may fear, or hope, or believe, according to our different principles) the English spirit is unacademic, an Academy would probably be impotent and perhaps ridiculous in England. But we can allow for this; and when we have allowed for it, once more Mr Arnold's warnings are warnings on the right side, true, urgent, beneficial. There are still the minor difficulties. Even at the time, much less as was known of France in England then than now, there were those who opened their eyes first and then rubbed them at the assertion that "openness of mind and flexibility of intelligence" were the characteristics of the French people. But once more also, no matter! The central drift is right, and the central drift carries many excellent things with it, and may be allowed to wash away the less excellent. Mr Arnold is right on the average qualities of French prose; whether he is right about the "provinciality" of Jeremy Taylor as compared to Bossuet or not, he is right about "critical freaks," though, by the way—but it is perhaps unnecessary to finish that sentence. He is right about the style of Mr Palgrave and right about the style of Mr Kinglake; and I do not know that I feel more especially bound to pronounce him wrong about the ideas of Lord Macaulay. But had he been as wrong in all these things as he was right, the central drift would still be inestimable—the drift of censure and contrast applied to English eccentricity, the argument that this eccentricity, if it is not very good, is but too likely to be very bad.

Yet it is perhaps in the illustrative essays that the author shows at his best. Even in the Guérin pieces, annoyance at the waste of first-rate power on tenth-rate people need not wholly blind us to the grace of the exposition and to the charming eulogy of "distinction" at the end. That, if Mr Arnold had known a little more about that French Romantic School which he despised, he would have hardly assigned this distinction to Maurice ; and that Eugénie, though undoubtedly a "fair soul," was in this not distinguished from hundreds and thousands of other women, need not matter very much after all. And with the rest there need be few allowances, or only amicable ones. One may doubt whether Heine's charm is not mainly due to the very lawlessness, the very contempt of "subject," the very quips and cranks and caprices that Mr Arnold so sternly bans. But who shall deny the excellence and the exquisiteness of this, the first English tribute of any real worth to the greatest of German poets, to one of the great poets of the world, to the poet who with Tennyson and Hugo completes the representative trinity of European poets of the nineteenth century proper ? Very seldom (his applause of Gray, the only other instance, is not quite on a par with this) does the critic so nearly approach enthusiasm — not merely *engouement* on the one side or serene approval on the other. No matter that he pretends to admire Heine for his " modern spirit " (why, *O Macarée*, as his friend Maurice de Guérin might have said, should a modern spirit be better than an ancient one, or what is either before the Eternal?) instead of for what has been, conceitedly it may be, called the " tear-dew and star-fire and rainbow-gold " of his phrase and verse. He felt this magic at any rate. No matter that he applies the wrong comparison instead of the right one, and depreciates French in order to exalt German, instead of thanking Apollo for these two good different things. The root of the matter is the right root, a discriminating enthusiasm : and the flower of the matter is one of the most charming critical essays in English. It is good, no doubt, to have made up one's mind about Heine before reading Mr Arnold ; but one almost envies those who were led to that enchanted garden by so delightful an interpreter.

Almost equally delightful, and with no touch of the sadness which must always blend with any treatment of Heine, is the next essay, the pet, I believe, of some very excellent judges, on " Pagan and Mediæval Religious Sentiment," with its notable translation of Theocritus and its contrast with St Francis. One feels, indeed, that Mr Arnold was not quite so well equipped with knowledge on the one side as on the other ; indeed, he never was well read in mediæval literature.

But his thesis, as a thesis, is capable of defence ; in the sternest times of military etiquette he could not have been put to death on the charge of holding out an untenable post ; and he puts the different sides with incomparable skill and charm. Mr Arnold glosses Pagan morals rather doubtfully, but so skilfully ; he rumples and blackens mediæval life more than rather unfairly, but with such a light and masterly touch !

Different again, inferior perhaps, but certainly not in any hostile sense inferior, is the "Joubert." It has been the fashion with some to join this essay to the Guérin pieces as an instance of some incorrigible twist in Mr Arnold's French estimates, of some inability to admire the right things, even when he did admire   I cannot agree with them. Joubert, of course, has his own shortcomings as a *pensée*-writer. He is *rococo* beside La Bruyère, dilettante beside La Rochefoucauld, shallow beside Pascal. There is at times, even if you take him by himself, and without comparison, something thin and amateurish and conventional about him. But this is by no means always or very often the case ; and his merits, very great in themselves, were even greater for Mr Arnold's general purpose.

That subtle and sensitive genius did not go wrong when it selected Joubert as an eminent example of those gifts of the French mind which most commended themselves to itself—an exquisite *justesse*, an alertness of spirit not shaking off rule and measure, above all, a consummate propriety in the true and best, not the limited sense of the word. Nor is it difficult to observe in the shy philosopher a temperament which must have commended itself to Mr Arnold almost as strongly as his literary quality, and very closely indeed connected with that—the temperament of equity, of *epieikeia*, of freedom from swagger and brag and self-assertion. And here, once more, the things receive precisely their right treatment, the treatment proportioned and adjusted at once to their own value and nature and to the use which their critic is intending to make of them. For it is one of the greatest literary excellences of the *Essays in Criticism* that, with rare exceptions, they bear a real relation to each other and to the whole—that they are not a bundle but an organism; a university, not a mob.

The subjects of the two last essays, *Spinoza* and *Marcus Aurelius*, may at first sight, and not at first sight only, seem oddly chosen. For although the conception of literature illustrated in the earlier part of the book is certainly wide, and admits — nay, insists upon, as it always did with Mr Arnold—considerations of subject in general and of morals and religion in particular, yet it is throughout one of literature as such. Now, we cannot say that the interest of Spinoza or that of Marcus Aurelius, great as it is in both cases, is wholly, or in the main, or even in any considerable part, a literary interest. With Spinoza it is a philosophical-religious interest, with Marcus Aurelius a moral-religious, almost purely. The one may indeed illustrate that attempt to

see things in a perfectly white light which Mr Arnold
thought so important in literature ; the other, that attention to conduct which he thought more important still.
But they illustrate these things in themselves, not in
relation to literature.   They are less literary even than
St Francis ; far less than the author of the *Imitation.*

It cannot therefore but be suspected that in including
them Mr Arnold, unconsciously perhaps, but more probably with some consciousness, was feeling his way
towards that wide extension of the province of the critic,
that resurrection of the general Socratic attitude, which
he afterwards adventured.   But it cannot be said that
his experiments are on this particular occasion in any
way disastrous.   With both his subjects he had the very
strongest sympathy — with Spinoza (as already with
Heine) as a remarkable example of the Hebraic spirit
and genius, rebellious to or transcending the usual
limitations of Hebraism ; with Marcus Aurelius as an
example of that non-Christian morality and religiosity
which also had so strong an attraction for him.   There
is no trace in either essay of the disquieting and almost
dismaying jocularity which was later to invade his discussion of such things: we are still far from Bottles; the
three Lord Shaftesburys relieve us by not even threatening to appear.   And accordingly the two essays add in
no small degree, though somewhat after the fashion of
an appendix or belated episode, to the charm of the
book.   They have an unction which never, as it so often
does in the case of Mr Arnold's dangerous master and

model Renan, degenerates into unctuosity; they are nobly serious, but without being in the least dull; they contain some exceedingly just and at the same time perfectly urbane criticism of the ordinary reviewing kind, and though they are not without instances of the author's by-blows of slightly unproved opinion, yet these are by no means eminent in them, and are not of a provocative nature. And I do not think it fanciful to suppose that the note of grave if unclassified piety, of reconciliation and resignation, with which they close the book, was intended—that it was a deliberate " evening voluntary " to play out of church the assistants at a most remarkable function—such a function as criticism in English had not celebrated before, such as, I think, it may without unfairness be said has not been repeated since. *Essays in Criticism*, let us repeat, is a book which is classed and placed, and it will remain in that class and place : the fresh wreaths and the fresh mud, that may be in turn unfitly thrown upon it, will affect neither.

Between this remarkable book and the later ones of the same *lustrum*, we may conveniently take up the thread of biography proper where we last dropped it. The letters are fuller for this period than perhaps for any other ; but this very fulness makes it all the more difficult to select incidents, never, perhaps, of the very first importance, but vying with each other in the minor biographical interests. A second fishing expedition to Viel Salm was attempted in August 1862 ; but it did not escape the curse which seems to dog attempts at repetition of the same pleasure. The river was hopelessly low ; the fish would not take ; and the traveller came back in very little more than " a day and a night and a morrow." By December danger-signals are up in a letter to his mother, to the effect that " it is intolerable absurdity to profess [who does?] to see Christianity through the spectacles of a number of second- or third-rate men who lived in Queen Elizabeth's time "—that time so fertile in nothing but the second-rate and the third. But it is followed a little later by the less disputable observation, " It is difficult to make out exactly at what [F. D.] Maurice is driving ; perhaps he is always a little dim in his own mind " on that point.

The illuminations at the Prince of Wales's marriage, where like other people he found " the crowd very good-humoured," are noted ; and the beginning of *Thyrsis* where and while the fritillaries blow. But from the literary point of view few letters are more interesting than a short one to Sir Mountstuart (then Mr) Grant Duff, dated May 14, 1863, in which Mr Arnold declines an edition of Heine, the loan of which was offered for his lecture—later the well-known essay. His object, he says, " is not so much to give a literary history of Heine's work as to mark his place in modern European letters, and the special tendency and significance of what he did." He will, therefore, not even read these things of Heine's that he has not read, but will take the *Romancero* alone for his text, with a few quotations from elsewhere. With a mere passing indication of the fact that

Matthew Arnold here, like every good critic of this
century, avowedly pursues that plan of " placing " writers
which some of his own admirers so foolishly decry, I
may observe that this is a *locus classicus* for his own
special kind of criticism.   It is possible—I do not know
whether he did so — that Sir Mountstuart may, on
receiving the letter, have smiled and thought of " Mon
siége est fait "; but I am sure he would be the first to
admit that the cases were different.   I do not myself
think that Mr Arnold's strong point was that complete
grasp of a literary personality, and its place, which
some critics aim at but which few achieve.   His im-
patience— here perhaps half implied and later openly
avowed—of the historic estimate in literature, would of
itself have made this process irksome to him.   But on
the lines of his own special vocation as a critic it was
not only irksome, it was unnecessary.   His function
was to mark the special—perhaps it would be safer to
say *a* special—tendency of his man, and to bring that
out with all his devices of ingenious reduplication,
fascinating rhetoric, and skilful parading of certain
favourite axioms and general principles.   This function
would not have been assisted— I think it nearly certain
that it would have been hampered and baulked—by
that attempt to find " the whole " which the Greek
philosopher and poet so sadly and so truly declares that
few boast to find.   It was a side, a face, a phase of each
man and writer, that he wished to bring out; and,
though he might sometimes exaggerate this, yet his ex-

aggeration was scarcely illegitimate. To bring out something he had to block out much. If he had attempted
to show the whole Goethe, the whole Heine, the whole
Homer or Shakespeare even, they would have been
difficult if not impossible to group and to compare in
the fashion in which he wished to deal with them.

And except on the sheer assumption, which is surely
a fallacy, that *suppressio veri* is always and not
only sometimes *suggestio falsi*, I do not see that he ex-
ceeded a due licence in this matter, while that he was
wise in his generation there can be no doubt. He
wanted to influence the average Englishman, and he
knew perfectly well there is nothing the average Englishman dislikes so much as guarded and elaborately con-
ditioned statements. The immense popularity and
influence of Macaulay had been due to his hatred of
half-lights, of " perhapses "; and little as Mr Arnold
liked Macaulay's fiddle, he was wise enough to borrow
his rosin, albeit in disguise. If a critic makes too
many provisos, if he " buts " too much, if he attempts to
paint the warts as well as the beauties, he will be
accused of want of sympathy, he will be taxed with
timorousness and hedging, at best he will be blamed for
wire-drawn and hair-splitting argument. The preambles
of exposition, the conclusions of summing up, will often
be considered tedious or impertinent. The opposite
plan of selecting a nail and hitting that on the head
till you have driven it home was, in fact, as much
Mr Arnold's as it was Macaulay's. The hammer-play

of the first was far more graceful and far less monotonous : yet it was hammer - play all the same. But
we must return to our *Letters*.

A dinner with Lord Houghton—"all the advanced
Liberals in religion and politics, and a Cingalese in full
costume "—a visit to Cambridge and a stroll to Grant-
chester, notice of about the first elaborate appreciation
of his critical work which had appeared in England, the
article by the late Mr S. H. Reynolds in the *Westminster Review* for October 1863, visits to the Roths-
childs at Aston Clinton and Mentmore, and interesting
notices of the composition of the *Joubert*, the *French
Eton*, &c., fill up the year. The death of Thackeray
extracts one of those criticisms of his great contemporaries which act as little douches from time to time, in
the words, "I cannot say that I thoroughly liked him,
though we were on friendly terms : and he was not to
my mind a great writer." But the personal reflections
which follow are of value. He finds "the sudden cessation of so vigorous an existence very sobering. To-
day I am forty-one ; the middle of life in any case, and
for me perhaps much more than the middle. I have
ripened and am ripening so slowly that I should be glad
of as much time as possible. Yet I can feel, I rejoice
to say, an inward spring which seems more and more to
gain strength and to promise to resist outward shocks,
if they must come, however rough. But of this inward
spring one must not talk [it is only to his mother that
he writes this] for it does not like being talked about,

and threatens to depart if one will not leave it in mystery."

An interview with Mr Disraeli at Aston Clinton, not, as one may suppose, without pleasant words, opens 1864. " It is only from politicians who have themselves felt the spell of literature that one gets these charming speeches," he says, and they, not unnaturally, charmed him so much that he left his dressing-case and his umbrella behind him. But the anti-crusade is more and more declared. He " means to deliver the middle-class out of the hand of their Dissenting ministers," and in the interval wants to know how " that beast of a word ' waggonette ' is spelt ? " The early summer was spent at Woodford, on the borders of Epping Forest, and the early autumn at Llandudno, where Welsh scenery and the poetry of the Celtic race " quite overpower" him. Alas ! some other poetry did not, and when we find him in September thinking *Enoch Arden* " perhaps the best thing Tennyson has done," we are not surprised to find this remarkable special appreciation followed by a general depreciation, which is quite in keeping. He is even tempted (and of course asked) to write a criticism of the Laureate, but justly replies, " How is that possible ? "

From 1865 we get numerous notices of the notices of the *Essays*, and a pleasant and full account of a second official tour on the Continent, with special dwellings at most of the Western and Central European capitals. The tour lasted from April to November, and I have sometimes thought that it might, by itself, give a better idea of Mr Arnold as an epistoler than the *Letters* at large seem to have given. Early in 1866 we hear of the beginnings of the *Friendship's Garland* series, though the occasion for that name did not come till afterwards. And he spent the summer of that year (as he did that of the next) in a farmhouse at West Humble, near Dorking, while he caught "*a* salmon" in the Deveron during September.

The occasion is perhaps a good one to say a few words on the relations between Mr Arnold and M. Renan, though the latter is not so prominent in the Continental letters as Sainte-Beuve and M. Scherer are. The author of the *Vie de Jésus* was a very slightly younger man than Mr Arnold (he was born in 1823), but in consequence of his having left the seminary and begun early to live by literary work, he was somewhat in advance of his English compeer in literary repute. His contributions to the *Débats* and the *Revue des Deux Mondes* began to be collected soon after 1850, and his first remarkable single book, *Averroès et l'Averroïsme*, dates from that year. I do not know how early Mr Arnold became acquainted with his written work. But they actually met in 1859, during the business of the Foreign Education Commission, and there is a very remarkable passage in a letter to Mrs Forster on Christmas Eve of that year. He tells his sister of "Ernest Renan, a Frenchman I met in Paris," and notes the considerable resemblance between their lines of endeavour, observing, however, that Renan is chiefly "trying to inculcate morality, in a high sense

of the word, on the French," while *he* is trying to inculcate intelligence on the English. After which he makes
a long and enthusiastic reference to the essay, *Sur la
Poésie des Races Celtiques*, the literary results of which we
shall soon see. I do not know whether Mr Arnold ever
expressed to his intimates—for the reference to M.
Renan in "Numbers" is not quite explicit—what he
thought of those later and very peculiar developments of
"morality in a high sense of the word" which culminated
in the *Abbesse de Jouarre* and other things. His sense
of humour must have painfully suggested to him that his
own familiar friend and pattern Frenchman had become
one of the most conspicuous examples of that French
lubricity which he himself denounced. But there was
no danger of his imitating M. Renan in this respect. In
others the following was quite unmistakable, and, I am
bound to say, on the whole rather disastrous. In literary criticism Mr Arnold needed no teaching from M.
Renan, and as his English training on one of its sides preserved him from the Frenchman's sentimental hedonism,
so on another it kept him from the wildest excesses
of M. Renan's critical reconstructions of sacred history.
But he copied a great deal too much of his master's
dilettante attitude to religion as a whole, and, as we shall
see, he adopted and carried a great deal further M.
Renan's (I am told) not particularly well-informed and
(I am sure) very hazardous and fantastic ideas about
Celtic literature. On the whole, the two were far too
much alike to do each other any good. Exquisite even

as M. Renan's mere style is, it is exquisite by reason of
sweetness, with a certain not quite white and slightly
phosphorescent light, not by strength or by practical
and masculine force. Now it was the latter qualities
that Mr Arnold wanted ; sweetness and light he could
not want.

As the tenure of his Chair drew to a close, and as
he began to loathe examination papers more and more
(indeed I know no one to whom *usus concinnat amorem*
in the case of these documents), he made some en-
deavours to obtain employment which might be, if not
both more profitable and less onerous, at any rate one
or the other. First he tried for a Charity Commissionership ; then for the librarianship of the House of Com-
mons. For the former post it may be permitted to
think that his extremely strong — in fact partisan —
opinions, both on education and on the Church of
England, were a most serious disqualification ; his appointment to the latter would have been an honour to
the House and to England, and would have shown that
sometimes at any rate the right man can find the right
place. But he got neither. He delivered his last Oxford lecture in the summer term of 1867. I remember
that there were strong undergraduate hopes that Mr
Browning, who was an Honorary M.A., might be got to
succeed him ; but it was decided that the honorary
qualification was insufficient, and I daresay there were
other objections. Mr Arnold had a sort of "send-off"
in the shape of two great dinners at Balliol and Merton,

at which he and Mr Browning were the principal guests, and the close of his professorial career was further made memorable by the issue of the *Study of Celtic Literature* in prose and the *New Poems* in verse, with *Schools and Universities on the Continent* to follow next year. Of these something must be said before this chapter is closed.

On the Study of Celtic Literature is the first book of his to which, as a whole, and from his own point of view, we may take rather serious objections. That it has merits not affected by these objections need hardly be said ; indeed I think it would not be foolish to say that it is — or was — even the superior of the *Homer* in comparative and indirect importance. In that Mr Arnold had but, at the best, roused men to enter upon new ways of dealing with old and familiar matter ; in this he was leading them to conquest of new realms. Now, as we have seen, it was exactly this exploration, this expansion, of which English was then in most need, just as it is now perhaps in most need of concentration and retreat upon the older acquisitions.

So far so good ; but if we go farther, we do not at first fare better. It would be grossly unjust to charge Mr Arnold with all the nonsense which has since been talked about Celtic Renascences ; but I fear we cannot write all that nonsense off his account. In particular, he set an example, which has in this and other matters been far too widely followed, of speaking without sufficient knowledge of fact.

It cannot be too peremptorily laid down that the literary equivalent of a "revoke" — the literary act after which, if he does it on purpose, you must not play with a man—is speaking of authors and books which he has not read and cannot read in the original, while he leaves you ignorant of his ignorance. *This* Mr Arnold never committed, and could never have committed. But short of it, and while escaping its penalty, a man may err by speaking too freely even of what he confesses that he does not know; and of this minor and less discreditable sin, I own (acknowledging most frankly that I know even less of the *originals* than he did), I think Mr Arnold was here guilty.

Exactly how much Gaelic, Irish, or Welsh Mr Arnold knew at first-hand, I cannot say: he frankly enough confesses that his knowledge was very closely limited. But what is really surprising, is that he does not seem to have taken much trouble to extend it at second-hand. A very few Welsh triads and scraps of Irish are all that, even in translation, he seems to have consulted : he never, I think, names Dafydd ap Gwilym, usually put forward as the greatest of Celtic poets ; and in the main his citations are derived either from *Ossian* ("this do seem going far," as an American poetess observes), or else from the *Mabinogion*, where some of the articles are positively known to be late translations of French - English originals, and the others are very uncertain. You really cannot found any safe literary generalisations on so very small a basis of such very shaky matter. In fact, Mr Arnold's argument for the presence of "Celtic magic," &c., in Celtic poetry comes to something like this. "There is a quality of magic in Shakespeare, Keats, &c.; this magic must be Celtic: therefore it must be in Celtic poetry." Fill up the double enthymeme who list, I am not going to endeavour to do so. I shall only say that two sentences give the key-note of the book as argument. "Rhyme itself, all the weight of evidence tends to show, came into our poetry from the Celts." Now to some of us all the weight of evidence tends to show that it came from the Latins. "Our only first-rate body of contemporary poetry is the German." Now at the time (1867), for more than thirty years, Germany had not had a single poet of the first or the second class except Heine, who, as Mr Arnold himself very truly says, was not a German but a Jew.

But once more, what we go to Mr Matthew Arnold for is not fact, it is not argument, it is not even learning. It is phrase, attitude, style, that by which, as he says admirably in this very book, "what a man has to say is recast and heightened in such a manner as to add dignity and distinction to it." It is the new critical attitude, the appreciation of literary beauty in and for itself, the sense of "the word," the power of discerning and the power of reflecting charm, the method not more different from the wooden deduction of the old school of critics than from the merely unenlightened and Philistine commonness of the reviewers, his earlier contemporaries, or from the aimless " I like that " and " I don't like this " which does duty now, and did then, and has done always, for criticism itself. True, Mr Arnold himself might be wilful, capricious, haphazard ; true, he might often be absolutely unable to give any real reason for the faith that was in him ; true, he sometimes might have known more than he did know about his subject. But in all these points he saved himself: in his wilfulness, by the grace and charm that sometimes attend caprice ; in his want of reason, by his genuineness of faith itself ; in his occasional lack of the fullest knowledge, by the admirable use — not merely display — which he made of what knowledge he had. There may be hardly a page of the two books of his lectures in which it is not possible to find some opportunity for disagreement—sometimes pretty grave disagreement ; but I am sure that no two more valuable books, in their kind and subject, to their country and time, have been ever issued from the press.

The *New Poems* make a volume of unusual importance in the history of poetical careers. Mr Arnold lived more than twenty years after the date of their publication ; but his poetical production during that time filled no more than a few pages. At this date he was a man of forty-five—an age at which the poetical

impulse has been supposed to run low, but perhaps
with no sufficient reason. Poets of such very different types as Dryden and Tennyson have produced
work equal to their best, if not actually their best,
at that age and later. Mr Browning had, a few years
before, produced what are perhaps his actually greatest
volumes, *Men and Women* and *Dramatis Personæ*, the
one at forty-three, the other at fifty-two. According
to Mr Arnold's own conception of poetry-making, as
depending upon the subject and upon the just and
artist-like exposition of that subject, no age should be
too late.

Certainly this age was not too late with him. The
contents all answered strictly enough to their title,
except that *Empedocles on Etna* and some half-dozen
of its companions were, at Mr Browning's request,
reprinted from the almost unpublished volume of
1852, and that *Thyrsis, St Brandan, A Southern
Night*, and the *Grande Chartreuse* had made magazine appearances. Again the moment was most important. When Mr Arnold had last made (omitting
with an apology the "transient and embarrassed
phantom" of *Merope*) an appearance in 1855, the
transition age of English nineteenth-century poetry
was in full force. No one's place was safe but
Tennyson's; and even his was denied by some, including Mr Arnold himself, who never got his eyes
quite clear of scales in that matter. Browning, though
he had handed in indisputable proofs, had not yet had

them allowed ; the Spasmodics had not disappeared ; the great præ-Raphaelite school was but on the way. The critics knew not what to think ; the vulgar thought (to the tune of myriad copies) of Tupper. Both classes, critic and public, rent *Maud* and neglected *Men and Women : The Defence of Guenevere* had not yet rung the matins - bell in the ears of the new generation.

Now things were all altered. The mixture of popularity and perfection in the *Idylls* and the *Enoch Arden* volume—the title poem and *Aylmer's Field* for some, *The Voyage* and *Tithonus* and *In the Valley of Cauterets* for others—had put Tennyson's place

" Beyond the arrows, shouts, and views of men."

The three-volume collection of Browning's *Poems*, and *Dramatis Personæ* which followed to clench it, had nearly, if not quite, done the same for him. *The Defence of Guenevere* and *The Life and Death of Jason*, *Atalanta, Chastelard*, and most of all the *Poems and Ballads*, had launched an entirely new poetical school with almost unexampled pomp and promise on the world. The Spasmodics were forgotten, the Tupper cult had been nearly (not yet quite) laughed out of existence. That Mr Arnold's own poems had had any widely extended sale or reading could hardly be said ; but they were read by those who were or were shortly to be themselves read. You had not to look far in any Oxford college (I cannot speak of Cambridge) before you found them on those undergraduate shelves which mean so much; while many who, from general distaste to poetry or from accident, knew them not, or hardly knew them, were familiar with their author's prose work, or at least knew him as one whom others knew.

The volume itself was well calculated to take advantage, to at least a moderate extent, of this conjunction of circumstance. At no time was the appeal of Mr Arnold's poetry of the most impetuous or peremptory order. And it might be contended that this collection contains nothing quite up to the very best things of the earlier poems, to the *Shakespeare* sonnet, to *The Scholar-Gipsy*, to the *Isolation* stanzas. But with the majority of its readers it was sure rather to send them to these earlier things than to remind them thereof, and its own attractions were abundant, various, and strong.

In the poet himself there was perhaps a slight consciousness of " the silver age." The préfatory *Stanzas*, a title changed in the collected works to *Persistency of Poetry*, sound this note—

> " Though the Muse be gone away,
>   Though she move not earth to-day,
>   Souls, erewhile who caught her word,
>   Ah ! still harp on what they heard."

A confession perhaps a little dangerous, when the Muses were speaking in no uncertain tones not merely to juniors like Mr Morris and Mr Swinburne but to seniors like Tennyson and Browning. But the actual contents were more than reassuring. Of *Empedocles* it is not necessary to speak again : *Thyrsis* could not but charm. The famous line,

> " And that sweet city with her dreaming spires,"

sets the key dangerously high ; but it is kept by the magnificent address to the cuckoo,

> " Too quick despairer, wherefore wilt thou go ? "

and the flower-piece that follows ; by that other single masterpiece,

> " The coronals of that forgotten time ; "

by the more solemn splendour of the stanza beginning

> " And long the way appears which seemed so short ; "

by the Signal tree ; and by the allegoric close with the reassertion of the Scholar. All these things stand by themselves, hold their sure and reserved place, even in the rush and crowd of the poetry of the sixties, the richest, perhaps, since the time from 1805 to 1822.

Saint Brandan, which follows, has pathos if not great power, and connects itself agreeably with those Celtic and mediæval studies which had just attracted and occupied Mr Arnold. The sonnets which form the next division might be variously judged. None of them equals the *Shakespeare ;* and one may legitimately hold the opinion that the sonnet was not specially Mr Arnold's form. Its greatest examples have always been reached by the reflex, the almost combative, action of intense poetic feeling—Shakespeare's, Milton's, Wordsworth's, Rossetti's — and intensity was not Mr Arnold's characteristic. Yet *Austerity of Poetry*, *East London*, and *Monica's Last Prayer* must always stand so high in the second class that it is hardly critical weakness to allow them the first. And then the tide rises. *Calais Sands* may not be more than very pretty, but it is that, and *Dover Beach* is very much more. Mr Arnold's theological prepossessions and assumptions may appear in it, and it may be unfortunately weak as an argument, for except the flood itself nothing is so certain a testimony to the flood as the ebb. But the order, the purpose, the argument, the subject, matter little to poetry. The expression, the thing that is *not* the subject, the tendency outside the subject, which makes for poetry, are here, and almost of the very best. Here you have that passionate interpretation of life, which is so different a thing from the criticism of it ; that marvellous pictorial effect to which the art of line and colour itself is commonplace and *banal*, and which prose literature never attains except by a *tour de force ;* that almost more marvellous accompaniment of vowel and consonant music, independent of the sense but reinforcing it, which is the glory of English poetry among all, and of nineteenth-century poetry among all English, poetries. As is the case with most Englishmen, the sea usually inspired Mr Arnold — it is as natural to great English poets to leave the echo of the very word ringing at the close

of their verse as it was to Dante to end with "stars."
But it has not often inspired any poet so well as this,
nor anywhere this poet better than here. If at any
time a critic may without fatuity utter judgment with
some confidence, it is where he disagrees with the
sentiment and admires the poem; and for my part I
find in *Dover Beach*, even without the *Merman*, without
the *Scholar-Gipsy*, without *Isolation*, a document which
I could be content to indorse "Poetry, *sans phrase*."

The Terrace at Berne has been already dealt with,
but that mood for epicede, which was so frequent in
Mr Arnold, finds in the *Carnac* stanzas adequate, and
in *A Southern Night* consummate, expression. *The
Fragment of Chorus of a Dejaneira*, written long before, but now first published, has the usual faults of
Mr Arnold's rhymeless verse. It is really quite impossible, when one reads such stuff as—

> " Thither in your adversity
> Do you betake yourselves for light,
> But strangely misinterpret all you hear.
> For you will not put on
> New hearts with the inquirer's holy robe
> And purged considerate minds "—

not to ask what, poetically speaking, is the difference
between this and the following—

> " To college in the pursuit of duty
> Did I betake myself for lecture ;
> But very soon I got extremely wet,
> For I had not put on
> The stout ulster appropriate to Britain,
> And my umbrella was at home."

But *Palladium*, if not magnificent, is reconciling, the Shakespearian *Youth's Agitations* beautiful, and *Growing Old* delightful, not without a touch of terror. It is the reply, the *verneinung*, to Browning's magnificent *Rabbi ben Ezra*, and one has almost to fly to that stronghold in order to resist its chilling influence. But it is poetry for all that, and whatever there is in it of weakness is redeemed, though not quite so poetically, by *The Last Word*. The *Lines written in Kensington Gardens* (which had appeared with *Empedocles*, but were missed above) may be half saddened, half endeared to some by their own remembrance of the "black-crowned red-boled" giants there celebrated—trees long since killed by London smoke, as the good-natured say, as others, by the idiotic tidiness of the gardeners, who swept the needles up and left the roots without natural comfort and protection. And then, after lesser things, the interesting, if not intensely poetical, *Epilogue to Lessing's Laocoon* leads us to one of the most remarkable of all Mr Arnold's poems, *Bacchanalia, or the New Age*. The word remarkable has been used advisedly. *Bacchanalia*, though it has poignant and exquisite poetic moments, is not one of the most specially *poetical* of its author's pieces. But it is certainly his only considerable piece of that really poetic humour which is so rare and delightful a thing. And, like all poetic humour, it oscillates between cynicism and passion almost bewilderingly. For a little more of this what pages and pages of jocularity

about Bottles and the Rev. Esau Hittall would we
not have given! what volumes of polemic with the
Guardian and amateur discussions of the Gospel of
St John! In the first place, note the metrical struc-
ture, the sober level octosyllables of the overture
changing suddenly to a dance - measure which, for a
wonder in English, almost keeps the true dactylic
movement. How effective is the rhetorical iteration of

> " The famous orators have shone,
>   The famous poets sung and gone,"

and so on for nearly half a score of lines! How perfect
the sad contrast of the refrain—

> " *Ah! so the quiet was!*
>   *So was the hush!*"

how justly set and felicitously worded the rural picture
of the opening! how riotous the famous irruption of the
New Agers! how adequate the quiet moral of the end,
that the Past is as the Present, and more also! And
then he went and wrote about Bottles!

" Progress," with a splendid opening—

> " The master stood upon the mount and taught—
>   He saw a fire in his disciples' eyes,"—

conducts us to two other fine, though rhymeless, dirges.
In the first, *Rugby Chapel*, the intensity of feeling
is sufficient to carry off the lack of lyrical accomplishment. The other is the still better *Heine's Grave*,
and contains the famous and slightly pusillanimous lines

about the "weary Titan," which are among the best known of their author's, and form at once the motto and the stigma of mid-century Liberal policy. And then the book is concluded by two other elegies—in rhyme this time—*The Stanzas written at the Grande Chartreuse* and *Obermann once more.* They are, however, elegies of a different kind, much more self-centred, and, indeed, little more than fresh variations on "the note," as I ventured to call it before. Their descriptive and autobiographic interest is great, and if poetry were a criticism of life, there is plenty of that of them.

The third book—*Schools and Universities on the Continent* (1868)—in which are put the complete results of the second Continental exploration—is, I suppose, much less known than the non-professional work, though perhaps not quite so unknown as the earlier report on elementary education. By far the larger part of it— the whole, indeed, except a "General Conclusion" of some forty pages—is a reasoned account of the actual state of matters in France, Italy, Germany, and Switzerland. It is not exactly judicial; for the conclusion— perhaps the foregone conclusion — obviously colours every page. But it is an excellent example (as, indeed, is all its author's non - popular writing) of clear and orderly exposition—never arranged *ad captandum*, but also never "dry." Indeed there certainly are some tastes, and there may be many, to which the style is a distinct relief after the less quiet and more mannered graces of some of the rest.

Opinions may differ more as to the value of the book as a lesson, or as an argument. Mr Arnold had started with a strong belief in the desirableness—indeed of the necessity—of State-control of the most thoroughgoing kind in education; and he was not at all likely to miss the opportunity of fetching new weapons from the very arsenals and *places d'armes* of that system. He was thoroughly convinced that English ways generally, and especially the ways of English schools and colleges, were wrong; and he had, of course, no difficulty in pointing triumphantly to the fact that, if the institutions of Continental countries differed in some ways from each other, they all differed in nearly the same way from ours. It may undoubtedly be claimed for him— by those who see any force in the argument — that events have followed him. Education, both secondary and university in England, *has* to a large extent gone since on the lines he indicates; the threatened superiority of the German bagman has asserted itself even more and more; the "teaching of literature" has planted a terrible fixed foot in our schools and colleges. But perhaps the weight usually assigned to this kind of corroboration is rather imaginary. That a thing has happened does not prove that it ought to have happened, except on a theory of determinism, which puts "conduct" out of sight altogether. There are those who will still, in the vein of Mephistopheles-Akinetos, urge that the system which gave us the men who pulled us out of the Indian Mutiny can stand comparison with

the system which gave France the authors of the
débâcle ; that the successes of Germany over France
in war have no necessary connection with education,
and those of Germany over England in commerce,
diplomacy, &c., still less. They will even go further
— some of them — and ask whether the Continental
practices and the Arnoldian principles do not necessi-
tate divers terribly large and terribly ill-based assumptions, as that all men are *educable*, that the value of
education is undiminished by its diffusion, that all, or
at least most, subjects are capable of being made educational instruments, and a great many more.

On the other hand, they will cheerfully grant that
Mr Arnold never succumbed to that senseless belief in
examination which has done, and is doing, such infinite
harm. But they will add to the debit side that the
account of English university studies which ends the
book was even at the time of writing so inaccurate as
to be quite incomprehensible, unless we suppose that
Mr Arnold was thinking of the days of his own youth,
and not of those with complete accuracy. He says "the
examination for the degree of bachelor of arts, which we
place at the end of our three years' university course, is
merely the *Abiturienten-examen* of Germany, the *épreuve
du baccalauréat* of France, placed in both those countries
at the entrance to university studies " ; and it is by this
that he justifies Signor Matteucci's absurd description of
Oxford and Cambridge as *hauts lycées*. Now, in the
first place, there is not one single word in this sentence,

or in the context, or, so far as I remember, in the whole book, about the Honours system, which for very many years before 1868 had exalted the standard infinitely higher in the case of a very large proportion of men. And in the second place, there is not a word about the Scholarship system, which in the same way had for very many years provided an entrance standard actually higher—far higher in some ways—than the *concluding* examinations of the French *baccalauréat*. My own days at Oxford were from 1863 to 1868, the year of Mr Arnold's book. During that time there were always in the university some 400 men who had actually obtained scholarships on this standard ; and a very considerable number who had competed on it, and done fairly. Whether Mr Arnold shared Mark Pattison's craze about the abolition of the pass-man altogether, I do not know. But he ought to have known, and I should think he must have known, that at the time of his writing the mere and sheer pass-man—the man whose knowledge was represented by the minimum of Smalls, Mods, and Greats—was, if not actually in a minority,—in some colleges at least he was that—at any rate in a pretty bare majority. With his love of interference and control, he might have retorted that this did not matter, that the university *permitted* every one to stick to the minimum. But as a matter of fact he suggests that it provided no alternative, no *maximum* or *majus* at all.

By the time that we have now reached, that of his giving up the professorship, Mr Arnold's position was, for good and for evil, mostly fixed. When he took up the duties of his chair he was, though by no means a very young man and already the author of much remarkable work, yet almost unknown out of Oxford and a small official circle in London. He had now, at forty-five, not exactly popularity, but a very considerable, and a very lively and growing, reputation. By far the most and the best of his poetry was written; but it was only just coming to be at all generally read or at all justly appreciated. He had, partly in obeying, and partly in working against his official superiors, acquired a distinct position as an educational reformer. He had become something of a figure in society. But, above all, he had proclaimed with undoubting authority, and had ex-emplified with remarkable and varied skill, a new or at least a very greatly altered kind of literary criticism. And this had already threatened incursions into domains from which men of letters as such had generally kept aloof, or which, if they had touched, they had touched not as men of letters. Something of Socrates, something of Addison, something of Johnson, mingled in Mr Arnold's presentation of himself as, if not exactly an arbiter, at any rate a suggester of elegances in all things, poetry and politics, prose and polite manners, public thought, public morality, religion itself. These pretensions, if urged in a less agreeable manner, would have been intolerable; they were not universally tolerated as it was: but the gifts and graces of the critic made them —so far—inoffensive, even rather fascinating, to all save the least accommodating or the most clear-sighted, and to some even of these.

And we must remember that this appearance of Mr Arnold as the mild and ingenious tamer of the ferocious manners of Britons coincided with far wider and more remarkable innovations.   This was the time, at home, of the second Parliamentary Reform, which did at least as much to infringe the authority of his enemy the Philistine, as the first had done to break the power of the half-dreaded, half-courted Barbarian.   This was the time when, abroad, the long-disguised and disorganised power of Germany was to rearrange the map of Europe, and to bring about a considerable rearrangement of Mr Arnold's own ideas as to the respective greatness of foreign nations.   And finally the walls of another stronghold of British Philistia, its intense and apparently impregnable self-satisfaction with Free-trade and cheap money and so forth, were tottering and crumbling.   A blast against them — indeed a series of blasts from *Chartism* to the *Latter-day Pamphlets*—had been blown long before by Carlyle, in very different tones from Mr Arnold's.   They had lost their stoutest champion and their most eloquent panegyrist in Macaulay.   But Sadowa and household suffrage gave the final summons, if not the final shake.   Mr Arnold had done his best to co-operate ; but his object, to do him justice, was to be rather a raiser of the walls of Thebes than an over-thrower of those of Jericho, or even of Ashdod.   He set about, in all seriousness, to clear away the rubbish and begin the re-edification; unluckily, in but too many cases, with dubious judgment, and by straying into quarters where he had no vocation. But he never entirely neglected his real business and his real vocation, and fortunately he returned to them almost entirely before it was too late.

CHAPTER IV.

IN THE WILDERNESS.

THAT the end of Mr Arnold's tenure of the Professorship of Poetry was a most important epoch in his life
is sufficiently evident. In the ten years that came to
an end then, he had, as two such extremely competent
judges as Mr Disraeli and Crabb Robinson in different
ways told him,[1] passed from comparative obscurity into

[1] Mr Disraeli's words (in 1864) have been referred to above (p.
100). They were actually : "At that time [when they had met at
Lord Houghton's some seven or eight years earlier] . . . you your-
self were little known. Now you are well known. You have made
a reputation, but you will go further yet. You have a great future
before you, and you deserve it." Crabb Robinson was a much older
acquaintance, and is credited, I believe, with the remark far earlier,
that "he shouldn't *dare* to be intimate " with so clever a young man
as Matthew Arnold. Very shortly before his death in February
1867, he had met Mr Arnold in the Athenæum, and asked " which
of all my books I should myself name as the one that had got me
my great reputation. I said I had not a great reputation, upon which
he answered : 'Then it is some other Matthew Arnold who writes
the books.'" The passage, which contains an odd prophecy of the
speaker's own death, and an interesting indication that Mr Arnold
rightly considered the *Essays* to be "the book that got him his
reputation," will be found in *Letters*, i. 351.

something more than comparative prominence. His chair had been for him a real *cathedra*, and his deliverances from it had always assumed, and had at length, to a great extent, achieved, real authority. In criticism it was evident that if he had not revealed positively novel aspects of truth, he had formulated and put on record aspects which were presenting themselves to many, nay, most, of the best critical minds of his day. His criticism had drawn his poetry with it, if not into actual popularity, yet into something like attention. His attempts to obtain some other employment less irksome, less absorbing, and more profitable, had indeed been unsuccessful ; but he was rising in his own department, and his work, if still in part uncongenial and decidedly laborious, appears to have been much less severe than in earlier days. Partly this work itself, partly his writings, and partly other causes had opened to him a very large circle of acquaintance, which it was in his own power to extend or contract as he pleased. His domestic life was perfectly happy, if his means were not very great : and his now assured literary position made it easy for him to increase these means, not indeed largely, but to a not despicable extent, by writing. The question was, " What should he write ? "

It is probably idle ever to wish that a man had done anything different from that which he has done. Without being a rigid Determinist, one may be pretty well convinced that the actual conduct is the joint result of

abilities, and of desires, and of opportunity to exercise
them, and that the man, had he really done otherwise,
would have been unsuccessful or unhappy or both. But
I fear that if I had been arbiter of Mr Arnold's fate at
this moment I should have arranged it differently. He
should have given us more poems—the man who, far
later, wrote the magnificent *Westminster Abbey* on such
a subject as Dean Stanley, had plenty more poetry in
his sack. And in prose he should have given us infinite
essays, as many as De Quincey's or as Sainte-Beuve's
own, and more than Hazlitt's, of the kind of the *Heine*
and the *Joubert* earlier, of the *Wordsworth* and the
Byron later. I can see no reason why, in the twenty-
one years' lease of life upon which he now entered, he
should not have produced a volume a-year of these,—
there are more than enough subjects in the various
literatures that he knew ; and though it is possible that
in such extended application his method might have
proved monotonous, or his range have seemed narrow,
it is not likely. To complete the thing, I should have
given him, instead of his inspectorship, a headship at
Oxford, for which, it seems to me, he was admirably
fitted. But *Dis aliter visum :* at least it seemed otherwise good to Mr Arnold himself as far as his literary
employments were concerned, and the gods did not
interfere.

We have seen that he had, some years before, conceived the ambitious idea of changing the mind of
England on a good many points by no means merely

literary; and he seems, not altogether unnaturally, to have thought that now was the time to apply seriously to that work. His tenure of the Oxford chair had given him the public ear; and the cessation of that tenure had removed any official seal of etiquette which it might have laid on his own lips. A far less alert and acute mind than his must have seen that the Reform troubles of 1866 and the "leap in the dark" of 1867 were certain to bring about very great changes indeed at home; and that the war of the first-named year meant the alteration of many things abroad. He at least thought—and there was some justification of a good many kinds for him in thinking—that intellectual changes, of importance equal to the political, were coming or come upon the world. And so for a time he seems to have grown rather cold towards the Muses, his earliest and always his truest loves. Social, political, and religious matters tempted him away from literature; and for a matter of ten years it can hardly be said that he had anything to do with her except to take her name in vain in the title of by far his worst, as it was by far his most popular, volume.

It has been hinted in a note on one of the early pages in this book that the secret of this unfortunate twist is at least partly to be found in the peculiar character of Mr Arnold's official employment. For nearly twenty years he had been constantly thrown into contact with the English Dissenters; and, far earlier than the time which we have reached, they seem not only, in familiar

phrase, to have "got upon his nerves," but to have
affected his brain.   He saw all things in Dissent—or,
at least, in the middle-class Philistine Dissenter.   His
Philistia is not in the least a true portrait of the average middle-class household thirty or forty years ago ;
though, I daresay (I have little direct knowledge), it is
not an unfair one of the average Dissenting middle-
class household.   The religion which Mr Arnold attacks is not the religion of the Church of England at
all, or only of what was even then a decaying and un-
influential part of it, the extremer and more intolerant
sect of the Evangelicals.   Once more, I cannot from
personal knowledge say whether this portrait was true
of Dissent, but I can believe it.

Now, to derive an idea of England from the English
Dissenter is and was absurd.   Politically, indeed, he
had only too much power between 1832 and 1866,
from the tradition which made Liberal politicians fond
of petting him.   Socially, intellectually, and to a great
extent religiously, he had next to no power at all.   To
take the average manager of a "British" school as
the average representative of the British nation was
the wildest and most mischievous of confusions.   Yet
this practically was the basis of Mr Arnold's crusade
between 1867 and 1877.

The First Blast of the Trumpet was, intentionally no
doubt, the last of the Oxford lectures, and for that very
reason a rather gentle and insinuating one.   *Culture
and its Enemies*, which was the origin and first part, so

to say, of *Culture and Anarchy*, carried the campaign begun in the *Essays in Criticism* forward ; but only in the most cautious manner, a caution no doubt partly due to the fact of the author's expressed, and very natural and proper, intention of closing his professorial exercises with the *bocca dolce*.   Still this is at least conceivably due to the fact that the boldest extension of the campaign itself had not definitely entered, or at least possessed, the author's mind.   A considerable time, indeed from July 1867 to January 1868, passed before the publication of the lecture as an article in the *Cornhill* was followed up by the series from the latter month to August, which bore the general title of *Anarchy and Authority*, and completed the material of *Culture and Anarchy* itself.   This, as a book, appeared in 1869.

It began, according to the author's favourite manner, which was already passing into something like a mannerism, with a sort of half - playful, half - serious battery against a living writer (in this case Mr Frederic Harrison), and with a laudatory citation from a dead one (in this case Bishop Wilson).   Mr Harrison had blasphemed " the cant about culture," and Mr Arnold protests that culture's only aim is in the Bishop's words, " to make reason and the will of God prevail."   In the first chapter, famous thenceforward in English literature by its title, borrowed from Swift, of " Sweetness and Light," we have the old rallyings of the *Daily Telegraph* and the *Nonconformist*.   Then the general view is laid down, and is developed in those that follow, but still with more of a political than a religious bent, and with the political bent itself chiefly limited to the social aspect.

"Doing as one Likes" scatters a mild rain of ridicule on this supposed fetich of all classes in England; and then, the very famous, if not perhaps very felicitous, nickname-classification of "Barbarian-Philistine-Populace" is launched, defended, discussed in a chapter to itself. To do Mr Arnold justice, the three classes are, if not very philosophically defined, very impartially and amusingly rallied, the rallier taking up that part of humble Philistine conscious of his own weaknesses, which, till he made it slightly tiresome by too long a run, was piquant enough. The fourth chapter, "Hebraism and Hellenism," coasts the sands and rocks (on which, as it seems to some, Mr Arnold was later to make shipwreck) very nearly in the title and rather nearly in the contents, but still with a fairly safe offing. The opposition might be put too bluntly by saying that "Hellenism" represents to Mr Arnold the love of truth at any price, and "Hebraism" the love of goodness at any price; but the actual difference is not far from this, or from those of knowing and doing, fear of stupidity and fear of sin, &c. We have the quotation from Mr Carlyle about Socrates being "terribly at ease in Zion," the promulgation of the word Renascence for Renaissance, and so forth. "Porro unum est necessarium," a favourite tag of Mr Arnold's, rather holds up another side of the same lesson than continues it in a fresh

direction; and then "Our Liberal Practitioners" brings
it closer to politics, but (since the immediate subject is
the Disestablishment of the Irish Church) nearer also
to the quicksands.   Yet Mr Arnold still keeps away
from them; though from what followed it would seem
that he could only have done so by some such *tour de
force* as the famous "clubhauling" in *Peter Simple*.
Had *Culture and Anarchy* stood by itself, it would
have been, though very far from its author's masterpiece, an interesting document both in regard to his
own mental history and that of England during the
third quarter of the century, containing some of his
best prose, and little, if any, of his worst sense.

But your crusader—still more your anti-crusader—
never stops, and Mr Arnold was now pledged to this
crusade or anti-crusade.   In October 1869 he began,
still in the *Cornhill*,—completing it by further instalments in the same place later in the year, and pub-
lishing it in 1870,—the book called *St Paul and Protestantism*, where he necessarily exchanges the mixed
handling of *Culture and Anarchy* for a dead-set at the
religious side of his imaginary citadel of Philistia.   The
point of at least ostensible connection — of real departure—is taken from the "Hebraism and Hellenism"
contrast of the earlier book; and the same contrast is
strongly urged throughout, especially in the *coda*, "A
Comment on Christmas."   But this contrast is gradually
shaped into an onslaught on Puritanism, or rather on
its dogmatic side, for its appreciation of "conduct" of

morality is ever more and more eulogised. As regards
the Church of England herself, the attack is oblique;
in fact, it is disclaimed, and a sort of a Latitudinarian
Union, with the Church for centre, and dogma left out,
is advocated. Another of our Arnoldian friends, the
"Zeit-Geist," makes his appearance, and it is more than
hinted that one of the most important operations of
this spirit is the exploding of miracles. The book is
perfectly serious—its seriousness, indeed, is quite evidently deliberate and laboured, so that the author
does not even fear to appear dull. But it is still
admirably written, as well as studiously moderate and
reverent; no exception can be taken to it on the score
of taste, whatever may be taken on the score of orthodoxy from the one side, where no doubt the author
would hasten to plead guilty, or on those of logic,
history, and the needs of human nature on the other,
where no doubt his "not guilty" would be equally
emphatic.

The case is again altered, and very unfortunately
altered, in the next, the most popular and, as has been
said, the most famous of the series—its zenith at once
and its nadir—*Literature and Dogma*. A very much
smaller part of this had appeared in magazine form;
indeed, the contents of *St Paul and Protestantism* itself
must have seemed odd in that shape, and only strong
sympathies on the part of the editor could have obtained admission for any part of *Literature and Dogma*.
Much of it must have been written amid the excitement

of the French-Prussian War, when the English public
was athirst for "skits" of all sorts, and when Mr
Arnold himself was "i' the vein," being engaged in
the composition of much of the matter of *Friendship's
Garland*.   *St Paul and Protestantism* had had two
editions in the same year (*Culture and Anarchy*, a far
better thing, waited six for its second), and altogether
the state of things was such as to invite any author to
pursue the triumph and partake the gale.   And he
might at first flatter himself that he had caught the
one and made cyclone-use of the other; for the book,
appearing at the end of 1872, with the date of 1873,
passed through three editions in that year, a fourth in
1874, and a fifth two years later.   It was thus by far
Mr Arnold's most popular book; I repeat also that it
is quite his worst.

That it was in hopelessly bad taste here and there—
in taste so bad that Mr Arnold himself later cut out
the most famous passage of the book, to which accordingly we need here only allude—can be denied by nobody except those persons who hold "good form" to
be, as somebody or other puts it, "an insular British
delusion of the fifties and sixties."   But this excision
of his and, I think, some others, besides the "citations
and illustrations" which he confesses to having excluded from the popular edition, may give us the welcome leave to deal very briefly with this side of the
matter in other respects also.   We may pass over the
fun which Mr Arnold had with Archbishop Thomson

(who, whatsoe'er the failings on his part, was at any rate a logician) on the theory of causation; with the University of Cambridge about *hominum divomque voluptas alma Venus* (I have forgotten what was the bearing of this joke, and it is probably not worth inquiring into); with the Bishop of Gloucester about the Personality of God; with the Athanasian Creed, and its "science got ruffled by fighting." These things, as "form," class themselves; one mutters something well known about *risu inepto*, and passes on. Such a tone on such a subject can only be carried off completely by the gigantic strength of Swift, though no doubt it is well enough in keeping with the merely negative and destructive purpose of Voltaire. It would be cruel to bring *Literature and Dogma* into competition with *A Tale of a Tub;* it would be more than unjust to bring it into comparison with *Le Taureau blanc.* And neither comparison is necessary, because the great fault of *Literature and Dogma* appears, not when it is considered as a piece of doubtful or not doubtful taste, but when it is regarded as a serious composition.

In the first place, the child-like fashion in which Mr Arnold swallowed the results of that very remarkable "science," Biblical criticism, has always struck some readers with astonishment and a kind of terror. This new La Fontaine asking everybody, "Avez-vous lu Kuenen?" is a lesson more humbling to the pride of literature than almost any that can be found. "The prophecy of the details of Peter's death," we are told in

Literature and Dogma, " is almost certainly an addition after the event, *because it is not at all in the manner of Jesus*." Observe that we have absolutely no details, no evidence of any sort whatever, outside the Gospels for the " manner of Jesus." It is not, as in some at least of the more risky exercises of profane criticism in a similar field, as if we had some absolutely or almost absolutely authenticated documents, and others to judge by them. External evidence, except for the mere fact of Christ's existence and death, we have none. So you must, by the inner light, pick and choose out of the very same documents, resting on the very same authority, what, according to your good pleasure, is " in the manner of Jesus," and then black-mark the rest as being not so. Of course, when Mr Arnold thus wrote, the method had not been pushed *ad absurdum*, as it was later by his friend M. Renan in the *Histoire d'Israël*, to the dismay and confusion of no less intelligent and un-orthodox a critic than his other friend, M. Scherer. But it is more or less the method of all Biblical criticism of this sort, and Mr Arnold follows it blindly.

Again, the chief bent of the book is to establish that " miracles do not happen." Alas ! it is Mr Arnold's unhappy lot that if miracles *do* happen his argument confessedly disappears, while even if miracles do not happen it is, for his purpose, valueless Like almost all critics of his class recently, especially like Professor Huxley in another division, he appears not to com-prehend what, to the believers in the supernatural, the supernatural means. He applies, as they all apply, the tests of the natural, and says, " Now really, you know, these tests are destructive." He says—he cannot prove —that miracles do not happen now ; his adversaries, if they were wise, would simply answer, " *Après* ?" Do any of them pretend to prescribe to their God that His methods shall be always the same, or that those methods shall stand the tests of the laboratory and the School of Charters ? that He shall give "a good title," like a man who is selling a house ? Some at least would rather not ; they would feel appallingly little interest in a Divinity after this sworn-attorney and chartered-accountant fashion, who must produce vouchers for all His acts. And further (to speak with reverence), the Divinity whom they *do* worship would be likely to answer Mr Arnold in the words of a prophet of Mr Arnold's own—

> " Du gleichst dem Geist den du begreifst,
> Nicht Mir ! "

But this is not all. There is not only begging of the question but ignoring of the issue. *Literature and Dogma*, to do it strict justice, is certainly not, in intention at any rate, a destructive book. It is meant, and meant very seriously, to be constructive—to provide a substitute for the effete religion of Hooker and Wilson, of Laud and Pusey, as well as for that of Baxter and Wesley and Mr Miall. This new religion is to have for its Jachin Literature—that is to say, a delicate æsthetic appreciation of all that is beautiful in Christianity and out of it; and for its Boaz Conduct—that is to say, a morality at least as rigid as that of the purest Judaism, though more amiable. If dogma is to be banished, so is anything like licence; and in the very book itself Mr Arnold formulated, against his once (and still partly) beloved France, something like that denunciation of her worship of Lubricity which he afterwards put more plainly still. Even Hellenism, the lauded Hellenism, is told to mend its ways (indeed there was need for it), and the Literature - without - Dogmatist will have to behave himself with an almost Pharisaic correctness, though in point of belief he is to be piously Sadducee.

Now this is all very pretty and very creditable, but it will not work. The goods, to use the vulgar but precise formula of English law, "are not of the nature and quality demanded by the purchaser." Nobody wants a religion of that sort. Conduct is good ; poetic appreciation is perhaps better, though not for the general. But then religion happens to be something different from either, though no doubt closely connected with both. Mr Arnold does not exactly offer us a stone for bread, but he does, like the benevolent French princess in the story, offer us pie-crust. Pie-crust is a good thing ; it is a close connection of bread ; but it will not do for a substitute, and, in addition, it is much more difficult for the general to obtain. Moreover, there is a serious, a historical, difficulty about Conduct *plus* poetic appreciation, but *minus* what we call religion. Mr Arnold, in a stately sonnet, has told us that Sophocles was his ideal as a life-philosopher who was also a poet. He knew, presumably, the stories told about Sophocles in Athenæus, and though these might be idle scandal, he knew far too much not to be aware that there is nothing intrinsically impossible about them. It would have been rather interesting to hear him fully on this subject. But he was too busy with expatiating on the sweet reasonableness of Jesus and "the *Aberglaube* of the Second Advent" to trouble himself with awkward matters of this kind at the moment.

It may be suspected, however, that he did trouble himself with them, or with something like them, afterwards. The book—a deliberate provocation—naturally found plenty of respondents, though I do not remember that any one smashed it, as, for instance, Dean Mansel could have done if he had been alive, or as Cardinal Newman could, had he been still in the fold. Mr Arnold was perhaps not less really disquieted by its comparative popularity. For he had quite enough of Phocion in him to feel, if not to say, that he must have said something at least ambiguous, when the multitude applauded. At any rate, though the ill-omened series did not cease, nothing further appeared in it which showed the tone of *Literature and Dogma*. Indeed, of the concluding volumes, *God and the Bible* and *Last Essays on Church and Religion*, the first is an elaborate and rather anxious apology, and the second a collection of diverse and comparatively "anodyne" essays. It is significant — as showing how much of the success of

Literature and Dogma had been a success of scandal—
that neither of these volumes enjoyed the least popularity. *God and the Bible* was never reprinted till the
popular edition of the series thus far in 1884 ; and *Last
Essays* was never reprinted at all, or had not been up
to the date of the invaluable *Bibliography* of the works.
Indeed the copies now, 1899, on sale appear to be of
the first edition.   This cool reception does not discredit
either Barbarians or Philistines or Populace.   There are
good things in the *Last Essays* (to which we shall
return), but the general effect of them is that of a
man who is withdrawing from a foray, not exactly
beaten, but unsuccessful and disgusted, and is trying
to cover his retreat by alarums and excursions.

God and the Bible tells much the same tale.   It
originally appeared by instalments in the *Contemporary
Review*, where it must have been something of a choke-
pear even for the readers of that then young and
thoughtful periodical.   Unless the replier has the vigour
of Swift, or at least of Bentley, the adroitness in fence of
Pascal, or at least of Voltaire, " replies, duplies, quad-
ruplies " are apt to be wofully tedious reading, and Mr
Arnold was rather a *veles* than a *triarius* of controversy.
He could harass, but he did not himself stand harassing very well ; and here he was not merely the object
of attacks from all sides, but was most uneasily conscious
that, in some cases at least, he did not wish his enemies
to destroy each other.   He had absolutely no sympathy
with the rabid anti-Christianity of Clifford, very little

with the mere agnosticism of Huxley; he wanted to be
allowed to take just so much Biblical criticism as suited
him and no more. He wished to prove, in his own
remarkable way, the truth and necessity of Christianity,
and to this wish the contradictions of sinners were too
manifold. One must be stony-hearted not to feel some
pity for him, as, just when he thinks he has evaded an
orthodox brick, the tile of a disbeliever in the Fourth
Gospel whizzes at him; or as, while he is trying to
patch up his romantic reconstructions of imaginary
Jewish history and religion, the push of some aggressive reviewer bids him make good his challenge to meta-
physical theologians. But this interest is only passing.

In the Preface there is indeed some of the old attempt
at liveliness. Professor Clifford himself, then dead, is
disposed of with a not ungraceful mixture of pity and
satire; Messrs Moody and Sankey are not unpleasantly
rallied; Satan and Tisiphone, Mr Ruskin and Sir Robert
Phillimore, once more remind one of the groves of
Blarney or the more doubtful chorus in the *Anti-Jacobin*.
But the apologist is not really light-hearted : he cannot
keep the more solemn part of his apologia out of the
Preface itself, and assures us that the story of Adam's
fall "is all a legend. It never really happened, any of
it." Again one asks Mr Arnold, as seriously as possible,
"How *do* you know that? On your own calculus, with
your own estimate of evidence, how is it possible for
you to know that? You may, on your principles, say
that you are insufficiently persuaded that it *did* happen;

but how can you, without preternatural revelation (the very thing you will not admit) say that it did *not?* Surely there is some want of intellectual seriousness in thus lightly ignoring every rule of law and logic, of history and of common-sense?"

But the embarrassment thus revealed naturally shows itself even more in the book itself, notwithstanding the fact that Mr Arnold expressly declines to reply to those who have attacked *Literature and Dogma* as anti-Christian and irreligious.   Not even by summarily banishing this not inconsiderable host can he face the rest comfortably : and he has to resort to the strangest reasons of defence, to the most eccentric invitation of reinforcements from afar.

The strangest of all these, the clearest proof in itself of flurry and sense of need, is exhibited in his summoning—of all wonderful things—of Comparative Philology to the rescue of Literature.   To rebut the criticism on his denial of a Personal God, he takes refuge in the ethnological meaning of Deus, which, it seems, is "Shining."   The poor plain mind, already staggered by Mr Arnold's private revelations as to what did *not* happen 6000 years ago (or earlier) in the garden of Eden, quite succumbs before this privilegium of omniscience. One had thought that the results of philology and etymology of this sort were extremely ingenious guesses, to be admitted in so far as they do not conflict with facts, and till the next guess comes, but nothing more.   Lo ! they are quoted as if they were on a par with "two and

two make four," or the law of Excluded Middle. We
may not take Moses and the prophets without proof,
but Curtius and Professor Max Müller may speak, and
we must but hear. And later, when Mr Arnold is trying
to cope with Descartes, he flies for refuge to "the roots
as, bhu, and *sta.*"

One is tempted rather to laugh at this ; but on some
sides it is very serious. That no God of any religion can
be more of a mere hypothesis than *as, bhu,* and *sta,* never
seems to have occurred to Mr Arnold for one moment,
nor that he was cutting the throat of his own argument.
We must not, however, fall into his own mistake and quad-
ruplicate to his duply. It may be sufficient to say that
the long defence of the Fourth Gospel which this book
contains is one of the oddest things in all literature.
What, on Mr Arnold's principles, it matters whether the
Fourth Gospel was written in the first century, the fourth,
or the fourteenth, it is impossible for the poor plain
mind to see. He will not have it as revelation, and as
anything else its date is quite immaterial.

The fact is that this severe censor of "learned
pseudo-science mixed with popular legend," as he
terms theology, appears to have no idea of the value
of evidence whatever. The traditional history of the
Bible is not even to be considered ; but a conjectural
reconstruction of it by a Dutch critic, without in the
older cases one jot or tittle of evidence outside the
covers of the Bible itself, deserves every respect, if not
reverent acceptance *en bloc.* Miracles are fictions, and

the scenes in the garden of Eden and at the Sepulchre never happened; but *as, bhu,* and *sta* are very solemn facts, and you can find out all about the Divinity, because the word Deus means (not " has been guessed to mean," but *means*) "Shining." That Shakespeare knew everything is much more certain than that miracles do not happen; and he certainly knew Mr Arnold's case if not Mr Arnold, when he introduced a certain main episode in *A Midsummer Night's Dream.* To frown on Oberon and caress Bottom is venial compared with the dismissal of the Bible as popular legend, and the implicit belief in *as, bhu,* and *sta.*

A wilfully hostile historian of Mr Arnold could not dwell too long on these unfortunate books, for the handles they present are infinite; but for my part I shall take leave to say little more about them. To ask, in the common phrase, whether they did any harm would be to beg the question in their own manner; to ask whether they produced any effect would lead us too far. They certainly expressed a prevalent tendency. Most fortunately Mr Arnold was allowed another ten years and more wherein to escape from the wilderness which yielded these Dead Sea fruits, and to till his proper garden once more. Yet we have not quite done with the other fruits themselves.

The actual finale, *Last Essays on Church* and *Religion*, was still less popular, was indeed the least popular of all his works, seeing that, as has been said above, it has never been reprinted. It is easy to understand this, for it is perhaps the only one of his books which can be definitely called dull. The apologetic tone noticeable in *God and the Bible* continues, but the apology is illustrated and maintained in an even less attractive manner. The Preface is perhaps the least dead part of the book ; but its line of argument shares, and perhaps even exaggerates, the controversial infelicity of this unfortunate series. Mr Arnold deals in it at some length with the comments of two foreign critics, M. Challemel-Lacour and Signor de Gubernatis, on *Literature and Dogma*, bringing out (what surely could have been no news to any but very ill-educated Englishmen) the fact of their surprise, not at his taking the Bible with so little seriousness, but at his taking it with any seriousness at all. And he seems never even to dream of the obvious retort : " Certainly. These men are at any rate 'thorough'; they are not dilettante dalliers between two opinions. They have got far beyond your half-way house and have arrived at their destination. We have no desire to arrive at the destination, and therefore, if you will excuse us, we decline to visit the half - way house." It is less surprising that he did not see the force of the objections of another critic, M. Maurice Vernes, to the equally illogical and unhistorical plan of arbitrarily selecting this utterance as that of " Jesus," and another, given by the same authority, as not that of " Jesus." A man, who was sensible of this paralogism, could never take Mr Arnold's views on Church and Religion at all.

But when we leave the Preface, even such faint liveliness as this deserts us. The text contains four (or five, the second being divided into two parts) essays, lectures, or papers, *A Psychological Parallel*, *Bishop Butler and the Zeit-Geist*, *The Church of England*, and *A Last Word on the Burials Bill*. All had appeared in *Macmillan's Magazine* or the *Contemporary Review* during 1876, while *Bishop Butler* had been delivered as two lectures at Edinburgh, and *The Church of England* as an address to the London Clergy at Sion College, during the spring of that year.

Over all there is a curious constraint, the evidence of a mood not very difficult to analyse, and in the analysis of which lies almost all the satisfaction or edification to be got out of the book. The writer, though by no means abandoning his own point of view, and even flattering himself that some *modus vivendi* is about to be established between himself and the more moderate supporters of the Church and of religion, betrays not merely the well-known self-excusing and self-accusing tone, but odd flashes of discontent and weariness — nay, even a fretfulness such as might have been that of a Moses at Rephidim who could not bring water out of the rock. *A Psychological Parallel* is an attempt to buttress the apologia by referring to Sir Matthew Hale's views on witchcraft, to Smith, the Cambridge Platonist and

Latitudinarian, and to the *Book of Enoch* (of which, by
the way, it is a pity that Mr Arnold did not live to
see Mr Charles's excellent translation, since he desid-
erated a good one). Of course the argument is sun-
clear. If Hale was mistaken about witchcraft, St
Paul may have been mistaken about the Resurrection.
Expressions attributed to Christ occur in the *Book of
Enoch*, therefore they are not original and divine, &c.,
&c. And it would be out of place to attempt any reply
to this argument, the reply being in each case as sun-
clear as the argument itself. No believer in supernatural religion that I ever met considered Sir Matthew
Hale to have been inspired ; and no believer in the
divinity of Christ can fail to hold that His adoption of
words (if He did adopt them) makes them His.

The gist of the Butler lectures is considerably less
clear, and, if only for that reason, it cannot be suc-
cinctly stated or answered. In particular, it requires
rather careful " collection " in order to discover what
our friend the Zeit-Geist has to do in this galley. I
should imagine that, though an Edinburgh audience is
by no means alarmed at philosophy, the majority,
perhaps the enormous majority, of Mr Arnold's hearers
must have had a singularly dim idea as to his exact
drift. Indeed I cannot say that after reading the piece
when it first appeared, and again, twenty years later,
for the purposes of this book, I have any very distinct
notion of that drift myself. If it merely means that
Butler, being an eighteenth-century person, was afflicted

with the eighteenth - century limitations by the Zeit-Geist, eighty-six pages, and an imposing German compound at the head of every other one of them, seem a good deal for telling us this.   If it is a sort of indirect attack upon—an oblique demurrer to—Butler's constructive - aggressive orthodoxy in psychology and religion, one is bound to say with all politeness, first, that it is a case of *impar congressus*, and secondly, that the adventurous knight does not give himself a fair chance.   It will take more than eighty-six not very large pages, and a German word at the top of the alternate ones, to do that!   In the opening sketch of Butler himself Mr Arnold could not but be agreeable and even delightful.   It gives us, indeed, most pleasant promise of work in this same good kind soon to follow ; but for the rest we grope till we find, after some seventy-three of the eighty-six, that what Mr Arnold wanted to say is that Butler did not handle, and could not then have handled, miracles and the fulfilment of prophecy satisfactorily.   Butler, like St Paul, is undoubtedly inconvenient for those who believe that miracles do not happen, and that prophecies were either not made or not fulfilled.   So he must be got rid of.   But whether he is got rid of,—whether Mr Arnold and the Zeit-Geist have put him on the shelf as a venerable but antiquated object,—that is another question.

The two remaining essays show us Mr Arnold, in his character of at least would-be practical statesman, dealing no longer with points of doctrine but with the affairs

of the Church as a political body. The circumstances
of the first—the address delivered at Sion College—had
a certain piquancy : whether they had also sweet reasonableness and an entire accordance with the fitness of
things is a question no doubt capable of being debated.
Me the situation strikes, I must confess, as a little
grotesque. The layman in the wide sense, the amateur,
always occupies a rather equivocal position when he
addresses experts and the profession ; but his position
is never so equivocal as when he doubles the part of
non-expert with that of candid friend. How Mr Arnold
succeeded in this exceedingly delicate attempt I do not
propose to examine at any length. He thought himself
that he had " sufficiently marked the way in which the
new world was to be reached." Paths to new worlds
are always interesting, but in reading, or rather re-reading, the sailing directions of this Columbus twenty years
after date, one may be a little disappointed. The sum
appears to be a somewhat Tootsian declaration that
things of general are of no consequence. The Church
is better than Dissent ; at least she would be so if she
dropped all her dogma, the greater part of her super-
stitions about the rights of property and " my duty to
my neighbour," and as much as possible of the barriers
which separate her from Dissent itself. A most moderate
eirenicon. Still less need be said of the Burials Bill
paper, which is a sort of appendix or corollary to
the Sion speech, at the end of which the subject had
been referred to. The particular question, in this

phase of it, has long ceased to burn, and one need not disturb the ashes.

We must now turn to the incursions of this time into politics, which, if not much happier, were more amusing. The chief monument of them is the long unreprinted *Friendship's Garland*, which has always had some fervent devotees, and is very characteristic. It so happened that the period when *Essays in Criticism*, combined with his Oxford Lectures, introduced Mr Arnold to the public, was the period of the first years of the *Pall Mall Gazette*, when that brilliant periodical, with the help of many of the original staff of the *Saturday Review*, and others, was renewing for the sixties the sensation of a new kind of journalism, which the *Saturday* itself had given to the fifties, while its form and daily appearance gave it even greater opportunities. As early as the summer of 1866, during the agitation into which the public mind had been thrown by the astounding rapidity and thoroughness of the Prussian successes in the Seven Weeks' War, Mr Arnold had begun a series of letters, couched in the style of *persiflage*, which Kinglake had introduced, or reintroduced, twenty years earlier in *Eothen*, and which the *Saturday* had taken up and widely developed. He also took not a few hints from Carlyle in *Sartor* and the *Latterday Pamphlets*. And for some years at intervals, with the help of a troupe of imaginary correspondents and *comparses* — Arminius von Thundertentronckh, Adolescens Leo of the *Daily Telegraph*, the Bottles family of wealthy Dissenters, with cravings for their deceased wife's sisters, as well as a large number of more or less celebrated personages of the day, introduced in their proper persons, and by their proper names — he instructed England on its own weakness, folly, and vulgarity, on the wisdom and strength of the Germans, on the importance of *Geist* and ideas, &c., &c. The author brought himself in by name as a simple inhabitant of Grub Street, victimised, bullied, or compassionately looked down upon by everybody ; and by this well-known device took licence for pretty familiar treatment of other people. When the greater crash of 1870 came, and the intelligent British mind was more puzzled, yet more *Prusso-mimic*, than ever, he supplemented these letters, framed or bound them up, as it were, with a moving account of the death of Arminius before Paris, and launched the whole as a book.

The letters had been much laughed over ; but I do not think the book was very widely bought—at any rate, its very high price during the time in which it was out of print shows that no large number was printed. Perhaps this cold welcome was not altogether so discreditable to the British public as it would have been, had its sole cause been the undoubted but unpalatable truths told by the writer. Either, as some say, because of its thick-hidedness, or, as others, because of its arrogant self-sufficiency, the British public has never resented these much. But, in the first place, the thing was a falsetto. Mr Arnold had plenty of wit

but not much humour; and after a time one feels that
Bottles and Leo & Co. may be, as Dousterswivel
says, "very witty and comedy," but that we should
not be altogether sorry if they would *go*.   Further,
the direct personalities—the worst instances concerned
Lord Elcho, Mr Frederic Harrison, and the late Mr
Sala—struck, and strike, some people as being not
precisely in good taste.   The constant allusions and
references to minor and ephemeral things and persons
were not of course then unintelligible, but they were
even then teasing.   In all these points, if *Friendship's
Garland* be compared, I will once more not say with
A Tale of a Tub, but even with the *History of John
Bull*, its weakness will come out rather strongly.

But this was not all.   It was quite evident—and it
was no shame and no disadvantage to him—that the
jester was endeavouring to urge a very serious earnest
behind, and by means of, his jest; that he was no
mere railer, or caviller, or even satirist, but a convinced
reformer and apostle.   Yet when we try to get at
his programme—at his gospel—there is no vestige of
anything tangible about either.   Not very many impar-
tial persons could possibly accept Mr Arnold's favourite doctrine, that the salvation of the people lies in
state-provided middle-class schools; and this was specially difficult in 1871, if they remembered how some
few years before Mr Arnold had been extolling the
state-provided middle-class schools of France.   While,
for the rest, a man might be (as many men were)

thoroughly dissatisfied with the part England had played abroad in Italy, in the American Civil War, in Denmark, in the war of 1866, in the war of 1870, and at home from 1845 onwards, and yet not be able for the life of him to discover any way of safety in *Friendship's Garland.*

Nor, to take with the *Garland* for convenience sake *Irish Essays,* 1882, the political book which closed this period with the political book that opened it, do we find things much better, even long after "the Wilderness" had been mostly left behind. There is indeed less falsetto and less flippancy ; perhaps Mr Arnold had silently learnt a lesson, perhaps the opportunities of regular essays in "three-decker" reviews—of a lay sermon to working men, of a speech at the greatest public school in the world—discouraged the playfulness which had seemed permissible in addressing a skittish young evening newspaper. But the unpracticalness— not in the Philistine but in the strictly scientific sense — is more glaring than ever, and there are other faults with it. Great part of *An Unregarded Irish Grievance* is occupied by a long-drawn-out comparison of England's behaviour to Ireland with that of Mr Murdstone and his friend and manager Quinion to David Copperfield. In the first place, one thinks wickedly of the gibe in *Friendship's Garland* about " Mr Vernon Harcourt developing a system of un-sectarian religion from the life of Mr Pickwick." In the second, one asks on what principles of literary art a comparison, not wholly improper as a mere illustration in passing, can be worked to death and turned inside out and upside down, for some twenty mortal pages.

And so in other places. Yet the worst faults are not in form but in substance. Minor contradictions do not matter, though in a copy of the book I have read there is a damaging comparison by some annotator between Mr Arnold's description of English Government at p. 4 and his rosy picture of education under Government at p. 107. This might happen to anybody, and is not fatal. What is fatal is that this censor of the "unideaed" has evidently himself no "ideas," no first principles, in politics at all. That, play what tricks you will, all possible politics come round either to the Rule of the One, the Rule of the Few, or the Rule of the Many, and that the consequences of these rules, differentiated a little but not materially by historical and racial characteristics, are as constant as anything commonly called scientific,— this never seems to have occurred to Mr Arnold at all. He did not fully appreciate Thackeray, and Thackeray died too soon to know very much of him. But I have always thought that, for a criticism of life possessing prophetic genius, the Chevalier Strong's wedding congratulations to Arthur Pendennis are almost uncanny as regards the Matthæan gospel. "Nothing," said the Chevalier, when he had established himself as agent to the Duke of Garbanzos, "is so important to the welfare of the household as *Good Sherry*." And so we find that the Irish question, like all others, will be solved by the substitution of State-governed for private middle-class schools, by the saturation of England with "ideas," by all our old friends.

The rest matches. Mr Arnold pooh-poohs the notion that Ireland, except by force, will never be blended with England ; it would be as sensible to say this " of Scotland, Wales, or Cornwall." He was not, I think, dead — he was certainly not dead long —when Wales actually did follow, less formidably, of course, in the path of Ireland, beginning with the Church, going on to the Land, and not distantly threatening the State. As usual he goes to his books. He quotes Goethe—a great man of letters, but perhaps the most pedantic of great men of letters except Milton —to prove that "the English are pedants." He quotes Burke—the unregenerate Irish Whig Burke, not the prophet whose tongue the French Revolution had touched as it opened his eyes—to tell us what to do with Ireland. But the main point in at least one of these essays, *The Incompatibles*, is again connected with *David Copperfield*. I have said that, from the merely literary point of view, the perpetual ringing of the changes on Creakle, Murdstone, Quinion — Quinion, Murdstone, Creakle—is inartistic and irritating. But from the philosophical and political point of view it is far worse. No Englishman with any sense of fact ever has taken, or could take, Dickens's characters as normal types. They are always fantastic exaggerations, full of genius occasionally, but as unlike actual reality as those illustrations by Cruikshank which are their nearest companions in the art of line. Of the three figures selected in particular, Creakle is a caricature; Murdstone, though not exactly that, is a repulsive exception; and Quinion is so mere a *comparse* or "super" that to base any generalisation on him is absurd. The dislike of the British public to be "talked book to" may be healthy or unhealthy; but if it takes no great heed of this kind of talking book, small blame to it! The same hopeless, not to say the same wilful, neglect of the practical appears throughout. Mr Arnold (to his credit be it said) had no great hopes of the Land Bill of 1881. But his own panaceas—a sort of Cadi-court for "bag-and-baggaging" bad landlords, and the concurrent endowment of Catholicism—were, at least, no better, and went, if it were possible, even more in the teeth of history.

It may be worth while (taking the usual chronological licence for the sake of logical coherence) to say a few words on the other political and quasi-political pieces reprinted with *Irish Essays*—the address to Ipswich working men, *Ecce Convertimur ad Gentes*, the Eton speech on *Eutrapelia*, and the ambitious *Future of Liberalism*.[1] The first is a curious but not very im-

---

[1] Of the remaining contents, the *Prefaces* of 1853-5 are invaluable, at least the first is, but this has been already noticed. Of *The French Play in London*, I am, perhaps, no good judge, as I take little interest in the acted drama. It is much occupied with the inferiority of French poetry, and especially of the poetry of

portant appeal to the lower class to educate the
middle, with episodic praises of "equality," "academies," and the like, as well as glances at a more
extensive system of "municipalisation," which, not to
the satisfaction of everybody, has come about since.
The second contains some admirable remarks on
classical education, some still more admirable protests
against reading about the classics instead of reading
the classics, and the famous discourse on *Eutrapelia*,
with its doctrine that "conduct is three-fourths of life,"
its denunciation of "moral inadequacy," and its really
great indications of societies dying of the triumph of
Liberalism and Conservatism respectively.   A discourse
quite admirable in intention, though if "heckling" had
been in order on that occasion, a sharp youth might
have put Mr Arnold in some difficulty by asking where
the canons of "moral adequacy" are written.

But *The Future of Liberalism*, which the Elizabethans
would have called a "cooling-card" after the Liberal
triumph of 1880, exhibits its author's political quiddity
most clearly.   Much that he says is perfectly true ;
much of it, whether true or not, is, as Mr Weller
observes, "wery pretty."   But the old mistake recurs
of playing on a phrase *ad nauseam* — in this case a
phrase of Cobbett's (one of the greatest of phrase-
makers, but also one of the chief of the apostles of

Hugo ; the inferiority of English civilisation, especially of the
middle class.   There are good things in it, but they are better
said elsewhere.   The rest needs no notice.

unreason) about "the principles of Pratt, the principles
of Yorke." It was, of course, a capital *argumentum
ad invidiam*, and Mr Arnold frankly adopted it.   He
compared himself to Cobbett—a compliment, no doubt ;
but one which, I fear, Cobbett, who hated nothing so
much as a university man, would not have appreciated.
Cobbett thought of nothing but the agricultural labourer's
"full belly"—at least this is how he himself put it ;
and it would have enforced Mr Arnold's argument and
antithesis had he known or dared to use it.   Mr Arnold
thought of nothing but the middle classes' empty mind.
The two parties, as represented by the rather small Lord
Camden and the rather great Lord Hardwicke, cared for
neither of these things—so "the principles of Pratt, the
principles of Yorke" comes in as a refrain.   To the
average Briton quotation is no more argument than,
on higher authority, is blank verse.   Still it might
do for ornament, if not for argument,—might help the
lesson and point it at least.   So we turn to the lesson
itself.   This "Liberal of the future," as Mr Arnold
styles himself, begins, with orthodoxy if not with
philosophy, by warning the Tories off entirely.   "They
cannot really profit the nation, or give it what it needs."
Perhaps ; but suppose we ask for a little reason, just a
ghost of a premiss or two for this extensive conclusion ?
There is no voice, neither any that answers.   And
then, the Tories dismissed with a wave to all but
temporary oblivion (they are to be allowed, it seems,
to appear from time to time to chasten Liberalism), our

prophet turns to Liberalism itself. It ought to promote "the humanisation of man in society," and it doesn't promote this. Ah! what a blessed word is "humanisation," the very equivalent, in syllables as in blessedness, of "Mesopotamia"! But when for the considerable rest of the essay we try to find out what humanisation *is*, why we find nothing but the old negative impalpable gospel, that we must "*dis*materialise our upper class, *dis*vulgarise our middle class, *dis*brutalise our lower class." "Om-m-ject and sum-m-m-ject!" "om-m-ject and sum-m-m-ject," in short, as that famous flash of Thomas Carlyle's genius discovered and summarised Coleridge, and with Coleridge the whole nineteenth century. A screed of jargon—a patter of shibboleth—and that is all. Never a thought for this momentous question—"May you not possibly—indeed most probably—in attempting to remove what you choose to consider as the defects of these classes, remove also what you acknowledge to be their virtues—the governing faculty of the upper class, the conduct and moral health of the middle, the force and vigour of the lower?" A momentous question indeed, and one which, as some think, has *got* something of an answer since, and no comfortable one!

I must apologise, and I do, for anything that may appear too polemical in this chapter. But the circumstances of the case made it almost as impossible, as it would have been uninteresting, to be merely recitative and colourless; and Mr Arnold's own ex-

ample gives ample licence. In particular, any one
who has had actual and close knowledge of the actual
progress of politics for many years may be pardoned
for speaking with some decision on the practice of
sitting at ease in Zion, and raying out curious observations on Barbarians and Eutrapelia and the character of Mr Quinion. We may have too little of such
things in English politics—no doubt for a good many
years before Mr Arnold's day we *had* too little of
them. But too much, though a not unpopular, is a
very clumsy and very unscientific antidote to too
little, and in Mr Arnold's own handling of politics,
I venture to think that there was too much of them
by a very great deal.

It is very pleasant to turn from the literary results
of this period, from the spectacle of Pegasus

" Stumbling in miry roads of alien art,"

and harnessing himself to all manner of unsuitable
vehicles, to the private history of the decade. This,
though sadly chequered by Mr Arnold's first domestic
troubles, was on the whole prosperous, was somewhat
less laborious than the earlier years, and was light-
ened by ever more of the social and public distrac-
tions, which no man entirely dislikes, and which—
to a certain extent and in a certain way—Mr Arnold
did not dislike at all. The changes of occupation
and of literary aim by the termination of the professorship coincided, as such things have a habit of

doing, with changes in place and circumstance. The
Chester Square house grew too small for the children,
and a move to Harrow was first meditated and then
achieved. A very pleasant letter to his mother, in
November 1867, tells how he was present at the
farewell dinner to Dickens on his departure for
America, how they wanted him (vainly) to come to
the high table and speak, and how Lord Lytton
finally brought him into his own speech. He adds
that some one has given him "a magnificent box of
four hundred Manilla cheroots" (he must surely have
counted wrong, for they usually make these things
in two-hundred-and-fifties or five-hundreds), welcome
to hand on, though he did not smoke himself. In
another he expresses the evangelical desire to " do
Mr Swinburne some good."

But in January 1868 his baby - child Basil died ;
and the intense family affection, which was one of his
strongest characteristics, suffered of course cruelly, as
is recorded in a series of touching letters to his sister
and mother. He fell and hurt himself at Cannon
Street, too, but was comforted by his sister with a
leading case about an illiterate man who fell into a
reservoir through not reading a notice. The Harrow
house became a reality at Lady Day, and at Midsummer he went to stay at Panshanger, and "heard
the word 'Philistine' used a hundred times during
dinner and 'Barbarian' nearly as often" (it must be
remembered that the "Culture and Anarchy" articles

were coming out now). This half-childish delight in such matters (like Mr Pendennis's "It's all in the papers, and my name too!") is one of the most fascinating things about him, and one of not a few, proving that, if there was some affectation, there was no dissimulation in his nature. Too many men, I fear, would have said nothing about them, or assumed a lofty disdain. In September he mentions to Mr Grant Duff a plan (which one only wishes he had carried out, letting all the "Dogma" series go κατ' οὖρον as it deserved) for "a sketch of Greek poetry, illustrated by extracts in harmonious prose." This would have been one of the few great literary histories of the world, and so Apollo kept it in his own lap. The winter repeated, far more heavily, the domestic blow of the spring, and Tom, his eldest son, who had always been delicate, died, aged sixteen only, at Harrow, where since the removal he had been at school. There is something about this in the *Letters ;* but on the great principle of *curæ leves*, less, as we should expect, than about the baby's death.

In February next year Mr Arnold's double repute, as a practical and official "educationist" and as a man of letters, brought him the offer of the care of Prince Thomas of Savoy, son of the Duke of Genoa, and grandson of Victor Emmanuel, who was to attend Harrow School and board with the Arnolds. The charge, though honourable and, I suppose, prof-

itable, might not have been entirely to the taste of
everybody ; but it seemed to Mr Arnold a new link
with the Continent, and he welcomed it.   The same
year saw a visit to Knebworth, and a very interesting
and by no means unsound criticism on that important
event in the life of a poet, the issue of the first collected edition of his poems.[1]   This was in two volumes,
and is now rather precious.   " It might be fairly
urged that I have less poetic sentiment than Tennyson, and less intellectual vigour and abundance than
Browning ; yet because I have perhaps more of a
fusion of the two than either of them, and have
more regularly applied that fusion to the main line
of modern development, I am likely enough to have

---

[1] A note on the contents of this and the subsequent collected editions may not be unwelcome ; for, as was always the case with him,
he varied them not a little.   This first collection was advertised
as comprehending "the First and Second Series of the Author's
Poems and the New Poems," but as a matter of fact half-a-dozen
pieces—including things as interesting as *A Dream* and *Stagirius*—
are omitted, though the fine *In Utrumque Paratus* reappears for the
first time as a consolation.   As reprinted in 1877, this collection
dropped *The Church of Brou* except the third part, and recovered
not only *Stagirius* and others but *The New Sirens*, besides giving,
for the first time in book-form, *Haworth Churchyard*, printed twenty-
two years before in *Fraser*.   A further reprint in 1881 restored the
whole *Church of Brou* and *A Dream*, and gave two or three small
additions, especially *Geist's Grave*.   The *three*-volume edition of
1885 also republished *Merope* for the first time, and added *Westminster Abbey* and *Poor Matthias*.   The *one*-volume edition of 1890
reproduced all this, adding *Horatian Echo* and *Kaiser Dead ;* it
is complete save for the two prize poems, and six or seven smaller
pieces.

my turn." One can only query whether poetry has anything to do with "modern development," and desiderate the addition to "sentiment" of "art." He seems to imply that Mr Gladstone personally prevented his appointment to a commissionership under the Endowed Schools Act. But the year ended with a complimentary reference from Mr Disraeli at Latimers about "Sweetness and Light."

In February 1870 the famous Persian cat Atossa (now in the most comfortable lap of all the gods or goddesses, with Hodge and Bona Marietta and Hinse of Hinsfeldt) makes her first appearance; and in June Mr Arnold received the Oxford D.C.L. He set it down to "a young and original sort of man, Lord Salisbury, being Chancellor"; and Lord Salisbury himself afterwards told him that "no doubt he ought to have addressed him as 'vir dulcissime et lucidissime.'" But though he was much pleased by his reception, he thought Lord Salisbury "dangerous," as being unliterary, and only scientific and religious in his tastes.

In December he had an amusing and (as it ended well) not unsatisfactory experience of the ways of Income Tax Commissioners. These gentlemen acted on even vaguer principles than those on which they once assessed a poor dramatic amateur, who had by accident received £6 "author's rights" for a week, at £300 per annum, on the sound arithmetical argument that there are fifty (indeed, there are fifty-two) weeks in a year, and that fifty times six is three hundred. They put Mr Arnold's literary profits at £1000, and he had to expostulate in person before they would let him down to £200, though he pathetically explained that "he should have to write more articles than he ever had done" to prevent his being a loser even at that. About the catastrophe of the *Année Terrible*, his craze for "righteousness" makes him a very little Pecksniffian—one thinks of the Tower of Siloam. But it is pleasant to hear that, early in 1871, they are arranging for him "a perfect district, Westminster and a small rural part near Harrow." So one hopes that the days of posting from shire to shire and subsisting on buns were over. He is interested about Deutsch (the comet of a season for his famous Talmud articles), receives the Commandership of the Crown of Italy for his services to Prince Thomas, and is proposed for the Middlesex magistracy, but (to one's sorrow) declines. There is fishing at Chenies (*vide* an admirable essay of Mr Froude's) in the early summer, a visit to Switzerland in the later, and in September "the pigs are grown very large and handsome, and experts advise their conversion into bacon." But Mrs Arnold "does not like the idea." Indeed this is the drawback of pig-keeping, which is otherwise a most fascinating pastime; but you can escape it, and unite pleasure with profit, by merely breeding the pigs and selling the litters young.

After this respite fate was again cruel. On February 16, 1872, Mr Arnold's second son died at Harrow, and again the reception of the blow and its effect are

marked by lesser voicefulness in the grief.   Yet one
phrase, " I cannot write his name without stopping to
look at it in stupefaction at his not being alive," is
equal to volumes.   The letters of this year are few, but
in September begins a correspondence of some interest
and duration with a French pastor, M. Fontanès.   Nor
does 1873 give much except description of a tour to
Italy, while in May the Arnolds moved from Harrow,
with its painful memories, to Cobham, which was Mr
Arnold's home for the rest of his life.   In September
he "shoots worse than ever" (*vide Friendship's Garland*) in the famous preserves of Six Mile Bottom, and
soon after his mother dies.   But it is not given to all
men not to be motherless till they themselves are fifty.
And 1874 is again rather barren, even such yield as it
gives being rather didactic and controversial, as for
instance in a letter to his sister, who had apparently
remonstrated with some vigour against the tone of
Literature and Dogma.   A pleasant letter to Miss
Kingsley on her father's death (1875) puts in good
evidence against the charge of grudging appreciation
of contemporaries which has often been brought
against Mr Arnold, and which some unguarded expressions, rather injudiciously published in other letters,
may seem to confirm.

Another in December contains an instance[1] of that dis-

---

[1] " I do not like the course for the History School at all ; nothing
but read, read, read, endless histories in English, many of them by
quite second-rate men ; nothing to form the mind as reading really

like to history, which long before its publication careful
students of his works had always noticed in him. The
fact is, that to a man of ideas, as Mr Arnold would
have liked to be called — a man of theories or of
crotchets, as in extending order of unkindness people
actually did call him — history must be an annoying
study. The things that ought to happen do not
happen, and the things that do happen have to be awk-
wardly explained away or hazardously ignored. His
almost pettish disgust for the historic estimate in literature itself may have either caused or been caused by
this more general dislike, and the dislike itself explains
the leniency with which he always regarded the sheer
guess-work of the Biblical critics. But it is possible
to sympathise with his disapproval of the divorce of
History and Law, which used to be united in the Oxford
schools. Together they made a discipline, inferior
indeed, but only inferior, to that of the great school
of *Literæ Humaniores*, the best intellectual training in
the world. When they are divided, it may be feared
that law becomes a mere technicality, if not a mere
bread-study, and that history is at once thin and vague.

But Clio must have made interest with Nemesis ; for,
but a page or two afterwards, this disregard of history
leads Mr Arnold into a very odd blunder. His French
friend, M. Fontanès, had thought of writing about

great authors forms it, or even to exercise it as learning a new
language, or mathematics, or one of the natural sciences exercises it."

Godwin, but Mr Arnold dissuades him. "Godwin," he says, "est intéressant, mais il n'est pas une source ; des courants actuels qui nous portent, aucun ne vient de lui." Godwin is the high priest of Anarchism ; he is our first Socialist philosopher ; he advocated no marriage, woman's rights, the abolition of religion. And *dans nos courants actuels rien ne vient de lui !* This was early in 1876, and later in the same year we have from him the singular judgment that George Sand, just dead, was " the greatest spirit in our European world from the time that Goethe departed." The chronicle may be appropriately closed for the time by mentioning that in the spring of 1877 Mr Arnold was approached with a view to his standing once more for the Poetry Chair, and declined. The invitation, however, was a sort of summons to him to go back to his proper work, and in effect, though doubtless not in intention, he had already obeyed it. "A French Critic on Milton," published in January 1877, is the first literary article of any importance that his bibliography records for the whole decade which we have surveyed in this chapter.

Note.—It is particularly unlucky that the *Prose Passages,* which the author selected from his works and published in 1879, did not appear later. It is almost sufficient to say that less than one-fourth of their contents is devoted to literature, all the rest to the " Dead Sea fruit." I have therefore said nothing about the book in the text. It is, however, a useful though incomplete and one-sided chresto-mathy of Mr Arnold's style from the formal point of view, illustrat-ing both his minor devices of phrase and the ingenious *ordonnance* of his paragraphs in building up thought and statement.

CHAPTER V.

THE LAST DECADE.

IT would be unhistorical to assert, and unphilosophical to assume, that in the change or reversion noted at the end of the last chapter, Mr Arnold had any consciousness of relinquishment, still more to hint any definite sense of failure on his part. He would probably have said (if any one had been impertinent enough to ask, and he had condescended to reply) that he had said his say, had shot his bolt, and might leave them to produce their effect. But that there was, if no repentance, a certain disgust, I cannot but believe. He must have seen — he almost acknowledges that he saw — that the work which he at least thought was conservative was being utilised by others in a purely destructive spirit ; he must have found himself in very unwelcome alliances ; and (which is worst of all to a delicate and sensitive spirit) he must constantly have found fools dotting his *i*'s and emphasising his innuendoes in their own clumsy and Philistine fashion. At any rate, it is purely historical to say that he did henceforward almost entirely change his main line of operation as to religious matters, and that though, as has been shown, he persisted, not too fortunately, in politics, his method of discussion in that likewise was altered. As we heard no more of the three Lord Shaftesburys, so Bottles and his unwelcome society were permitted to remain unchronicled. In the latter department seriousness came upon Mr Arnold ; in the former, if not a total, yet a general and certainly most welcome silence.

Most welcome : for he was voiceful enough on other and his proper subjects. " Falkland," which followed "A French Critic on Milton," in March in the *Fortnightly*, and " George Sand," which followed it, as has been said, in June in the *Nineteenth Century*, somewhat deserved the title (*Mixed Essays*) of the volume in which they were two years later reprinted. But the last essay of the year 1877, that on Mr Stopford Brooke's *Primer*, was, like the " French Critic," and even more than that, pure literature. " A French Critic on Goethe," which appeared in the *Quarterly Review* for January 1878, followed next. The other pieces of this year, which also, with one exception, appeared in *Mixed Essays*, were, with that exception, evidences of a slight but venial relapse, or let us say of convalescence not yet quite turned into health. " Equality " (*Fortnightly*, March 1878), "Irish Catholicism and British Liberalism" (*Fortnightly*, July 1878), and " Porro Unum est Necessarium " (*Fortnightly*, November 1878), were, if not of " the utmost last provincial band," yet not of the pure Quirites, the genuine citizens of the sacred city of Mr Arnold's thought : and he seceded from this latter in not a few of those estimable but unimportant Irish essays which have been noticed in the last chapter.

But the literary contents of *Mixed Essays* are very interesting, and the Johnson paper (really a preface to the six selected lives, which he edited for Messrs Macmillan in 1878) is a most excellent piece of work. His selection of the Lives is perhaps not quite unerring. For he ought surely to have given the " Cowley," with its (from his own point of view) invaluable *point de repère* in the estimate of the " metaphysicals." And he might have missed the "Swift," which, though extremely interesting as a personal study from its mixture of prejudice and constraint, its willingness to wound, and yet—not its fear but—its honest compunction at striking, is, for the purpose of the volume, misplaced. But he had a right to give what he chose : and his preface has points of the very highest value. The opening passage about the *point de repère* itself, the fixed halting-place to which we can always resort for fresh starts, fresh calculations, is one of the great critical *loci* of the world, and especially involves the main contribution of the nineteenth century to criticism if not to literature altogether. We may exalt, without very much doubt or dread, the positive achievements of the century of Tennyson and Browning, of Carlyle and Thackeray, of Heine and Hugo. But we have seen such strange revolutions in this respect that it may not do to be too confident. The glory of which no man can deprive our poor dying *siècle* is that not one, of all the others since history began, has taken such pains to understand those before it, has, in other words, so discovered and so utilised the value of *points de repère.* It may be that this value is, except in the rarest cases, all that a critic can ever pretend to—that he may be happy if, as few do, he reaches this. But in the formulation of the idea (for he did much more than merely borrow it from the French) Mr Arnold showed his genius, his faculty of putting

"What oft was thought but ne'er so well expressed."

And when a man does this in prose or in verse, in criticism or in creation, he has his reward—a reward that no man can take away, even if any one were disposed to try.

As a whole, *Mixed Essays* itself, which followed *Last Essays on Church and Religion* at an interval of two years, is an almost immeasurably livelier book than its predecessor, and to some judgments at least seems to excel that predecessor in solid value as much as in the graces. "Mixed" is perhaps not a strictly accurate title, for the volume consists of two halves, the contents of each of which are homogeneous enough, but which have next to nothing to do with each other. But even in the non-literary essays we are out of "The Wilderness" in its worst sense. Most of the essays had, as has

just been shown, appeared in different periodicals, while
"Equality" was also delivered as a lecture during the
years 1877 and 1878. The exception was the paper
called "Democracy," which he reprinted from his first
work on Foreign Schools in 1861, where it had appeared
as an Introduction. The juxtaposition is by no means
uninteresting or uninstructive, though perhaps it is not
entirely favourable to the idea of Mr Arnold's development as a *zoon politicon*. It has been said before that
his earliest political writing is a good deal less fantastic
and more sane than that of his middle period, and though
"the last of life for which the first was made" was now
restoring to him much of his power in this direction,
yet he was always much joined to idols in matters political. In grasp "Democracy" does not quite come up to
its rather ambitious title; and a moment's thought will
show why. In 1861 Democracy was a very academic
subject. All projects for further Parliamentary Reform
had failed utterly in England; and nobody dreamt of
what the next five or six years would bring. In France
there was what looked like a crushing military despotism :
in other Continental countries the repression which had
followed the outbreaks of 1848-49 was only just being
relaxed, or not relaxed at all. American democracy
had not had its second baptism of Civil War. The
favourite fancies about the respective *ethos* of aristocracy, of the middle-class, and of the lower do
indeed appear, but for the most part Mr Arnold
confines himself to the simple question of State in-

terference, for which in his own subject of education he was so anxious, and which he would gladly have seen extended. It has been more than once remarked already that he may justly be regarded as a politician of more seriousness than he has here been represented as possessing, if espousing the cause of the things which actually happen is taken as the criterion. For State interference has grown and is growing every day. But then it may be held—and as a matter of principle he would not himself have contested it— that a man's politics should be directed, not by what he thinks will happen, but by what he thinks ought to happen. And some of us, while not in love by any means with the middle-class Liberal ideas of 1830-1860, think that the saving grace of that day that is dead was precisely its objection to State interference.

"Equality," which follows, and which starts what might be called at the time of the book its contemporary interest, is much more far-reaching and of greater curiosity; indeed, it may perhaps be held to be the most curious, in a certain sense, of all its author's writings, and to give, in a not fully satisfactory but suggestive fashion, a key to his complex character which is supplied by no other of his essays. That there was (in no silly or derogatory sense of an often absurdly used word) a slightly un-English side to that character, few acute judges would deny. But its results, in the greater part of the works, are so diffused, and, as it were, subterranean, that they are difficult to extract and concentrate. Here we seem to get the spirit much nearer proof. For the Equality which Mr Arnold here champions is not English but French equality; not political and judicial equality before the law, but social equality enforced by the law. He himself admits, and perhaps even a little exaggerates, his attitude of *Athanasius contra mundum* in this respect, amassing with relish expressions, in the sense opposite to his own, from such representative and yet essentially diverse authorities as Lord Beaconsfield, Mr Gladstone, Sir Erskine May, Mr Froude, and Mr Lowe. Against them he arrays Menander and George Sand — a counter-championship not itself suggestive of Equality. This may be "only his fun"—a famous utterance which it is never more necessary to keep in mind than when speaking or writing of Mr Arnold, for his fun, such as it was, was pervading, and occasionally rather cryptic. But the bulk of the paper is perfectly serious. Social equality, and its compulsory establishment by a law against free bequest or by public opinion, these are his themes. He asserts that the Continent is in favour of them; that the English colonies, *ci-devant* and actual, are in favour of them; that the Greeks were in favour of them; that the Bible is in favour of them. He cites Mr Hamerton as to the virtues of the French peasant. He renews his old tilt at the manners of the English lower-middle class, at Messrs Moody and Sankey, at the great "Jingo" song of twenty

years ago (as to which, by the way, a modern Fletcher
of Saltoun might have something to say to-day), at the
Puritans, at Mr Goldwin Smith, at many things and
many persons.

I feel that history has given me at the moment
rather an unfair advantage over Mr Arnold here. One
could always pick plenty of holes in " Equality," could
suggest that the Greeks did not make such a very good
thing of it with their equality (which included slavery);
that the Biblical point is far from past argument; that
M. Zola, for instance, supplies an interesting commen-
tary on Mr Hamerton's rose-coloured pictures of the
French peasantry; that whatever Mr Arnold's own lot
may have been, others who have lived in small French
towns with the *commis voyageur* have not found his
manners so greatly superior to those of the English
bagman. But just at this moment, and, in fact, in an
increasing degree ever since Mr Arnold wrote, the
glorification of France has become difficult or impossible. Sir Erskine May, it seems, had warned him
in vain about the political effect of French Equality
even at that time : but one need not confine oneself to
politics. At the end of the nineteenth century France
has enjoyed the blessings of social equality, enforced by
compulsory division of estates, for a hundred years and
more. Perhaps equality has nothing to do with the
decadence of her literature, with that state of morals
which Mr Arnold himself deplored with almost Puritan
emphasis, with the state of religion which he holds up

as an awful example, fit to warn England to flee to the refuge of his own undogmatic *Nephelococcygia*, with the ineffable scandals of Panama and the Dreyfus case, with the mixture of blind illucidity and febrile passion which characterises the French press. Only, what is left? Where are the improvements due to this great influence? They are, according to Mr Arnold, in the amiable dignity of the French peasant and the polished refinement of the French middle-class. Frankly, one may prefer Hodge and Bottles.

"Irish Catholicism and British Liberalism" has less actuality, and, moreover, it belongs to a group of which enough has been said in reference to the *Irish Essays*. But "Porro Unum est Necessarium" possesses not merely an accidental but a real claim to fresh attention, not merely at the moment when there is at last some chance of the dream of Mr Arnold's life, the interference of the State in English secondary education, being realised, but because it is one of the expressions of that dream which was in his life so important. It consists partly of statistics and partly of a moan over the fact that, in the heat and heyday of Mr Gladstone's *levée en masse* against the Tory Government of 1874-80, the Liberal programme contained nothing about this darling object. And the superiority of France is trotted out again ; but it would be cruel to insist any more. Yet at last Mr Arnold becomes practical, and contends for pretty much the substance of present Secondary Education Reform schemes—limited inspection, qualification of masters, leaving certificates, &c. "It do not over-stimulate," to quote an author to whom Mr Arnold was shortly to devote much attention; but we leave the political or semi-political batch in considerably greater charity with the author than his prose volumes for years past had rendered possible.

No reserves, no allowances of the least importance are necessary in dealing with the rest of the volume. I do not think it fanciful to discern a sort of involuntary or rather unconscious "Ouf!" of relief in the first, the "Guide to English Literature," on the subject, as has been said, of Mr Stopford Brooke's always excellent and then novel *Primer*. A tribute to duty is, indeed, paid at starting: we are told sternly that we must not laugh (as it is to be feared too many of us did and do) at the famous boast of the French Minister, as to all the boys in France learning the same lesson at the same hour. For this was the result of State interference: and all the works of State interference are blessing and blessed. But, this due rite paid, Mr Arnold gives himself up to enjoyment, laudation, and a few good-natured and, for the most part, extremely judicious proposals for making the good better still. Even if this last characteristic were not present, it would be unjust to call the article a puff. Besides, are puffs so wholly bad? A man may be not very fond of sweets, and yet think a good puff now and then, a puff with its three corners just hot from the oven, full of jam, light, artistically frothed, to be a very pleasing thing. And, as I have said, Mr Arnold's review is much more than a puff. Once, indeed, there is even a hypercriticism, due to that slight want of familiarity with literary history proper which has been noticed more than once. Mr Arnold finds fault with Mr Brooke for adopting, as one of his chapter divisions, "from the Restoration to George III." He objects to this that "George III. has nothing to do with literature," and suggests "to the Death of Pope and Swift." This is a curious mistake, of a kind which lesser critics have often repeated. Perhaps George III. *had* nothing to do with literature ; but his accession immediately preceded, and may even, as the beginning of a pure English *régime*, have done something to produce, numerous appearances of the Romantic revival—Percy's *Reliques*, Hurd's *Essays*, Macpherson's *Ossian, The Castle of Otranto*, and others. The deaths of Pope and Swift have no such synchronism. They mark, indeed, the disappearance of the strongest men of the old school, but not the appearance of even the weakest and most infantine of the new. Still this, though interesting in itself, is a trifle, and the whole paper, short as it is, is a sort of *Nunc Dimittis* in a new sense, a hymn of praise for dismissal, not from but to work—to the singer's proper function, from which he has been long divorced.

"Falkland," which follows, is less purely literary, but yet closely connected with literature. One thinks with some ruth of its original text, which was a discourse on Falkland by that modern Lucius Cary, the late Lord Carnarvon—the most curious and pathetic instance of a man of the nineteenth century speaking of one who was almost his exact prototype, in virtues and graces as in weaknesses and disabilities of temperament, during the seventeenth. It would, of course, have been indecent for Mr Arnold to bring this parallel out, writing as he did in his own name and at the moment, and I do not find any reference to it in the *Letters ;* but I can remember how strongly it was felt at the time. His own interest in Falkland as the martyr of Sweetness and Light, of lucidity of mind and largeness of temper, was most natural, and its sources most obvious. It would be cruel, and is quite unnecessary, to insist on the too certain fact that, in this instance at any rate, these excellent qualities were accompanied by a distinct weakness of will, by a mania for sitting between two stools, and by that—it may be lovable, it may be even estimable—incapacity to think, to speak, to behave like a man of this world, which besets the conscientious idealist who is not a fanatic. On the contrary, let us not grudge Mr Arnold a hero so congenial to himself, and so little repulsive to any of us. He could not have had a better subject ; nor can Falkland ever hope for a *vates* better consecrated, by taste, temper, and ability, to sing his praises.

Then we are back again in pure literature, with the two notable *Quarterly* articles, already glanced at, on M. Scherer as " A French Critic on Milton " and " A French Critic on Goethe." There was a very strong sympathy, creditable to both, between the two. M. Scherer went

further than Mr Arnold in the negative character of his
views on religion; but they agreed as to dogma. His
literary criticism was somewhat harder and drier than
Mr Arnold's; but the two agreed in acuteness, lucidity,
and a wide, if not quite a thoroughgoing, use of the comparative method. Both were absolutely at one in their
uncompromising exaltation of "conduct." So that Mr
Arnold was writing quite *con amore* when he took up
his pen to recommend M. Scherer to the British public,
which mostly knew him not at that time.

But he did not begin directly with his main subject.
He had always, as we have seen, had a particular
grudge at Macaulay, who indeed represented in many
ways the tendencies which Mr Arnold was born to
oppose. Now just at this time certain younger critics,
while by no means championing Macaulay generally,
had raised pretty loud and repeated protests against
Mr Arnold's exaggerated depreciation of the *Lays* as
"pinchbeck"; and I am rather disposed to think that
he took this opportunity for a sort of sally in flank.
He fastens on one of Macaulay's weakest points, a point
the weakness of which was admitted by Macaulay himself—the "gaudily and ungracefully ornamented" (as its
author calls it) *Essay on Milton*. And he points out,
with truth enough, that its "gaudy and ungraceful
ornament" is by no means its only fault—that it is bad
as criticism, that it shows no clear grasp of Milton's
real merits, that it ignores his faults, that it attributes
to him qualities which were the very reverse of his

real qualities. He next deals slighter but still telling blows at Addison, defends Johnson, in passing, as only negatively deficient in the necessary qualifications, not positively conventional like Addison, or rhetorical like Macaulay, and then with a turn, itself excellently rhetorical in the good sense, passes to M. Scherer's own dealings with the subject. Thenceforward he rather effaces himself, and chiefly abstracts and summarises the "French Critic's" deliverances, laying special stress on the encomiums given to Milton's style. The piece is one of his most artfully constructed ; and I do not anywhere know a better example of ingenious and attractive introduction of a friend, as we may call it, to a new society.

The method is not very different in "A French Critic on Goethe," though Carlyle, the English "awful example" selected for contrast, is less maltreated than Macaulay, and shares the disadvantageous part with Lewes, and with divers German critics. On the whole, this essay, good as it is, seems to me less effective than the other ; perhaps because Mr Arnold is in less accord with his author, and even seems to be in two minds about that author's subject—about Goethe himself. Earlier, as we have partly seen, he had, both in prose and in verse, spoken with praise—for him altogether extraordinary, if not positively extravagant—of Goethe ; he now seems a little doubtful, and asks rather wistfully for "the just judgment of forty years," the calm revised estimate of the Age of Wisdom. But M. Scherer's estimate is in parts lower than he can bring himself to admit ; and this turns the final passages of the essay into a rather unsatisfactory chain of " I agree with this," " I do not agree with that." But the paper retains the great merit which has been assigned to its predecessor as a piece of ushering ; and that, we must remember, was what it was designed to be.

In " George Sand," which completes the volume, we have Mr Arnold no longer as harbinger of another, but in the character, in which after all he is most welcome, of speaker on his own account. His estimate of this prolific *amuseuse* will probably in the long-run seem excessive to the majority of catholic and comparative critics ; nor is it at all difficult to account for the excess. Mr Arnold belonged exactly to the generation to which in England, even more than in France, George Sand came as a soothing and sympathetic exponent of personal sorrows. Even the works of her " storm-and-stress " period were not too far behind them ; and her later calmer productions seem to have had, at least for some natures among the " discouraged generation of 1850 " (to which, as we have said, Mr Arnold himself by his first publications belonged), something of that healing power which he has assigned, in larger measure and with greater truth, to Wordsworth. A man is never to be blamed for a certain generous overvaluation of those who have thus succoured him ; it would be as just to blame him for thinking his mother more beautiful, his father wiser than they actually were.

And Mr Arnold's obituary here has a great deal of charm. The personal and biographical part is done with admirable taste, not a grain too much or too little of that *moi* so *haïssable* in excess, so piquant as a mere seasoning, being introduced : and the panegyric is skilful in the extreme. To be sure, Mr Hamerton reappears, and Mr Arnold joins in the chorus of delight because the French peasant no longer takes off his hat. Alas! there is no need to go to the country of *La Terre* to discover this sign of moral elevation. But the delusion itself is only another proof of Mr Arnold's constancy to his early ideas. And looking back on the whole volume, one is almost tempted to say that, barring the first *Essays in Criticism* itself, he had written no better book.

Before very long the skill in selecting and editing which had been first applied to Johnson's *Lives* found extended opportunities. Mr Arnold had much earlier, in the *Essays in Criticism*, expressed a wish that the practice of introducing books by a critical and biographical Essay, which had long been naturalised in France, and had in former times not been unknown in England, should be revived among us. His words had been heard even before he himself took up the practice, and for about the usual time—your thirty years is as a matter of fact your generation—it flourished and prospered, not let us hope to the great detriment of readers, and certainly to the modest advantage of the public man when vexed by want of pence.

Nor can it exactly be said to have ceased—though for
some years grumbles have been uttered. "Why," says
one haughty critic,—"why mar a beautiful edition of
So-and-so's works by incorporating with them this or
that man's estimate of their value?" "The publishers,"
says an inspired *communiqué*, "are beginning to recognise
that the public has no need of such things in the case of
works of established repute, of which there is nothing
new to be said." No doubt both these are genuine
utterances : no doubt the haughty critic would have
steadily refused to "mar" the book by *his* estimate if
he had been asked to do so ; no doubt the particular
firm of publishers were not in the least influenced by a
desire to save the ten, twenty, fifty, or a hundred
guineas which this or that man might have demanded
for saying nothing new.

But Mr Arnold did not agree with these severe folk.
He thought—and not a few good wits have thought
with him—not only that these Introductions are an
opportunity for men like himself, with original gifts of
thought and style, to display these gifts, but that the
mighty public, for all its knowledge of everything that
has been thought and said about everybody, might
find something new to it even in the observations of
lesser folk. As a matter of fact, of course, and neither
to talk nor to quote nonsense, the utility of such Introductions, even if moderately well done, is unmistakable.
Not one in a thousand of the probable readers of any
book has all the information which even a fairly

competent introducer will put before him ; not one in
a hundred knows the previous estimates of the author ;
not many possess that acquaintance with his whole
work which it is part of the business of the introducer
to acquire, and adjust for the better understanding
of the particular book.   Of course, if an Introduction is imperfectly furnished with fact and thought
and reading—if it is desultory, in bad taste, and so
forth — it had better not be there.   But this is only
saying that a bad Introduction is a bad thing, which
does not get us much beyond the intellectual edification of the niece of Gorboduc.   Unless the introducer is a boggler, the Introduction will probably do
good to those who want it and can be neglected by
those who don't ; while in the rarer and better cases
it will itself acquire, or even possess from the first, that
very value as a *point de repère* which Mr Arnold had discussed.   It will be good relatively and good in itself,
—a contribution at once to the literature of knowledge
and to the literature of power.

Of Mr Arnold's efforts in editing I may be permitted
to neglect his "intromittings" with Isaiah, for reasons
already sufficiently given.   In more hopeful matter
there are three examples which are not soon likely
to lose interest or value : the selection of his own
poems, that from Wordsworth, and that from Byron.
To the first the English habits of his own day did
not permit him to prefix any extensive Introduction,
and though the principle is sound, one is almost sorry

for the application. Neither Wordsworth nor Coleridge would have had any scruples in doing this, and
while Mr Arnold had the sense of the ludicrous which
Wordsworth lacked, he was less subject to disastrous
divagations than Coleridge. Still, the 1853 Preface
enables those who have some slight power of expansion to fill in what is wanted from the point of view
of purpose ; and the selection itself is quite excellent.
Almost the only things that, as a basis for a good
knowledge of the poet, one finds it necessary to
subjoin, are the beautiful *Resignation*, which Mr
Humphry Ward had the good taste to include in the
appendix to his *English Poets ;* and the curious, characteristic, and not much short of admirable *Dream*,
which in the earlier issues formed part of *Switzerland*, and should never have been excluded from it.
It is probably the best selection by a poet from his
own works that has ever been issued, and this is
saying not a little. Nor does one like Mr Arnold
less for his saying, reported either by Mr Ward or
Lord Coleridge, that he had rather have given *all*
the poems.

As for the " Wordsworth " and the " Byron," they
gain enormously by " this man's estimate of them,"
and do not lose by " this man's " selection. I have
had occasion, not once or twice only, and for purposes not invariably the same, to go through the
Wordsworth book carefully, side by side with the
complete poems, in order to see whether anything

has necessarily to be added. I really do not know what has, unless it be a few of the oases from the deserts of the *Excursion*, the *Prelude*, and the then not published *Recluse*. Wordsworth's real titles are put in once for all; the things by which he must stand or fall are there. The professor, the very thorough - going student, the literary historian, must go farther; the idle person with a love of literature will; but nobody need.

And the Introduction (for after all we can all make our selections for ourselves, with a very little trouble) is still more precious. I know few critical essays which give me more pleasure in reading and re-reading than this. Not that I agree with it by any means as a whole; but he is in the mere "Pettys" of criticism (it is true not many seem to get beyond) who judges a critical essay by his own agreement with it. Mr Arnold puts Wordsworth, as a poet and an English poet, far higher than I can put him. He is not so great a poet to my thinking as Spenser or Shelley; if it were possible in these competitions to allow weight for age, he is not as great a poet as Keats; I am sure he is not a greater poet than Tennyson; I cannot give him rank above Heine or Hugo, though the first may be some- times naughty and the second frequently silly or rhe- torical; and when Mr Arnold begins to reckon Molière in, I confess I am lost. When and where did Molière write poetry? But these things do not matter; they are the things on which reviewers exercise their "will

it be believed?" and on which critics agree to differ.
We may include with them the disparaging passage on
Gautier (of whom I suspect Mr Arnold knew little, and
whom he was not quite fitted to judge had he known
more) and the exaltation of "life" and "conduct"
and all the rest of it. These are the colours of the
regiment, the blazonry of the knight; we take them
with it and him, and having once said our say against
them, pass them as admitted.

But what is really precious is first the excellent
criticism scattered broadcast all over the essay, and
secondly, the onslaught on the Wordsworthians. They
might perhaps retort with a *tu quoque*. When Mr
Arnold attacks these poor folk for saying that Wordsworth's poetry is precious because its philosophy
is sound, we remember a certain Preface with its
"all depends on the subject," and chuckle a little, a
very little. But Mr Arnold is right here. No philosophy, no subject, will make poetry without poetical
treatment, and the consequence is that *The Excursion*
and *The Prelude* are, as wholes, not good poems at all.
They contain, indeed, passages of magnificent poetry.
But how one longs, how, as one sees from this essay,
Mr Arnold longed, for some mercury-process which
would simply amalgamate the gold out of them and
allow us to throw the dross down any nearest cata-
ract, or let it be blown away by any casual hurricano!

The Byron paper contains more disputable statements
—indeed the passage about Shelley, if it were quite

serious, which may be doubted, would almost disqualify Mr Arnold as a critic of poetry. But it is hardly less interesting, and scarcely at all less valuable. In the first place, it is a very great thing that a man should be able to admire both Byron and Wordsworth. Of a mere Byronite, indeed, Mr Arnold has even less than he has of a Wordsworthian pure and simple. He makes the most damaging admissions; he has to fall back on Goethe for comfort and confirmation; he is greatly disturbed by M. Scherer's rough treatment of his subject. In no essay, I think, does he quote so much from others, does he seem to feel it such a relief to find a backer, a somebody to fight with on a side point, a somebody (for instance Professor Nichol) to correct and gloss and digress upon while complimenting him. Mr Arnold is obviously not at ease in this Zion—which indeed is a Zion of an odd kind. Yet this very uneasiness gives to the *Essay* a glancing variety, a sort of animation and excitement, which are not common things in critical prelections. Nor, though one may think that Mr Arnold's general estimate of Byron is not even half as sound as his general estimate of Wordsworth, does the former appear to be in even the slightest degree insincere. Much as there must have been in Byron's loose art, his voluble inadequacy — nay, even in his choice of subject—that was repellent to Mr Arnold: much more as there must have been in his unchastened conduct, his flashy affectations, his lack of dignity, morality, *tenue* of every kind,—yet there were real links between them. Mr Arnold saw in Byron an ally, if not an altogether admirable or trustworthy ally, against the Philistine. He saw in him a link with general European literature, a check and antidote to the merely insular. Byron's undoubtedly "sincere and strong" dislike of the extreme Romantic view of literature was not distasteful to Mr Arnold. Indeed, in his own earlier poems there are not wanting Byronic touches and echoes, not so easy to separate and put the finger on, as to see and hear "confusedly." Lastly, he had, by that sort of reaction which often exhibits itself in men of the study, an obvious admiration for Force—the admiration which makes him in his letters praise France up to 1870 and Germany after that date—and he thought he saw Force in Byron. So that the *Essay* is written with a stimulating mingle-mangle of attraction and reluctance, of advocacy and admission. It is very far indeed from being one of his best critically. You may, on his own principles, "catch him out" in it a score of times. But it is a good piece of special pleading, an excellent piece of writing, and one of the very best and most consummate literary *causeries* in English.

In strict chronological order, a third example of these most interesting and stimulating Prefaces should have been mentioned between the "Wordsworth" and the "Byron"—the latter of which, indeed, contains a reference to it. This is the famous Introduction to Mr T. H. Ward's *English Poets*, which, in that work and in the second series of *Essays in Criticism*, where

it subsequently appeared, has perhaps had more readers
than any other of its author's critical papers. It contains, moreover, that still more famous definition of
poetry as " a criticism of life " which has been so
often attacked and has sometimes been defended. I
own to having been, both at the time and since, one
of its most decided and irreconcilable assailants. Nor
do I think that Mr Arnold would have much relished
the apology made, I think, by Mr Leslie Stephen
since his death, that its critics " mistake an epigram
for a philosophical definition." In the first place, the
epigrammatic quality is not clearly apparent ; and in
the second place, an epigram would in the particular
place have been anything but appropriate, while a
philosophical definition is exactly what was wanted.

Mr Arnold himself never attempted any such defence. He pleaded, with literal justice, that the
phrase " a criticism of life " was only part of his
formula, which adds, " under the conditions fixed
for such a criticism by the laws of poetic truth and
poetic beauty." But this does not make the matter
much better, while it shows beyond controversy that
it *was* a philosophical definition that he was attempting. It merely takes us round in a circle, telling us
that poetry is poetical, that the archdeacon performs
archidiaconal functions. And while it is not more
illuminative than that famous and useful jest, it has
the drawback of being positively delusive, which the
jest is not. Unless we are to assign some quite new

meaning to " criticism "—and the assignment of new
meanings to the terms of an explanation is the worst
of all explanatory improprieties—poetry is *not* a criticism of life. It may be a passionate interpretation of
life—that has seemed to some not a bad attempt at
the unachievable,—a criticism it cannot be. Prose
fiction may be and should be such ; drama may be
and should be such ; but not poetry. And it is especially unfortunate that such poetry as answers best to
the term is exactly that poetry which Mr Arnold liked
least. Dryden and Pope have much good and true
criticism of life : *The Vanity of Human Wishes* is magnificent criticism of life ; but Mr Arnold has told us
that Dryden and Pope and Johnson are but "classics
of our prose." That there is criticism of life *in* poetry
is true ; but then in poetry there is everything.

It would also, no doubt, be possible to pick other holes
in the paper. The depreciation of the "historic estimate," instead of a simple hint to correct it by the
intrinsic, is certainly one. Another is a distinct ar-
bitrariness in the commendation or discommendation
of the examples selected. No one in his senses
would put the *Chanson de Roland* on a level with
the *Iliad* as a whole ; but some among those people
who happen to possess an equal acquaintance with
Greek and Old French will demur to Mr Arnold's
assignment of an ineffably superior poetical quality to
one of the two passages he quotes over the other. So
yet again with the denial of " high seriousness " to

Chaucer. One feels disposed to enter and argue out a whole handful of not quite contradictory pleas, such as "He *has* high seriousness" (*vide* the "Temple of Mars," the beginning of the *Parliament of Fowls*, and many other places): "Why should he have high seriousness?" (a most effective demurrer); and "What *is* high seriousness, except a fond thing vainly invented for the nonce?"

But, as has so constantly to be said in reference to Mr Arnold, these things do not matter. He must have his catchwords: and so "criticism of life" and "high seriousness" are introduced at their and his peril. He must have his maintenance of the great classics, and so he exposes what I fear may be called no very extensive or accurate acquaintance with Old French. He must impress on us that conduct is three-fourths of life, and so he makes what even those who stop short of *latreia* in regard to Burns may well think mistakes about that poet likewise. But all the spirit, all the tendency, of the *Introduction* is what it ought to be, and the plea for the "real" estimate is as wholly right in principle as it is partly wrong in application.

It is well borne out by the two interesting articles on Gray and Keats which Mr Arnold contributed to the same work. In the former, and here perhaps only, do we find him putting his shoulder to the work of critical advocacy and sympathy with an absolutely whole heart. With Wordsworth, with Byron, with Heine, he was on points more or fewer at grave difference; though he affected to regard Goethe as a *magnus Apollo* of criticism and creation both, I think in his heart of hearts there must have been some misgivings; and it is impossible that he should not have known his fancy for people like the Guérins to be mere *engouement*. Gray's case was different. The resemblances between subject and critic were extraordinary. Mr Arnold is really an industrious, sociable, and moderately cheerful Gray of the nineteenth century; Gray an indolent, recluse, more melancholy Arnold of the eighteenth. Again, the literary quality of the bard of the *Elegy* was exactly of the kind which stimulates critics most. From Sainte-Beuve downwards the fraternity has, justly or unjustly, been accused of a tendency to extol writers who are a little problematical, who approach the second class, above the unquestioned masters. And there was the yet further stimulus of redressing wrongs. Gray, though a most scholarly poet, has always pleased the vulgar rather than the critics, and he had the singular fate of being dispraised both by Johnson and by Wordsworth. But in this paper of Mr Arnold's the wheel came full circle. Everything that can possibly be said for Gray—more than some of us would by any means indorse—is here said for him : here he has provided an everlasting critical harbour, into which he may retreat whensoever the popular or the critical breeze turns adverse.

And the Keats, less disputable in its general estimate, is equally good in itself, and specially interest-

ing as a capital example of Mr Arnold's polemic—*the*
capital example, indeed, if we except the not wholly
dissimilar but much later article on Shelley's *Life*.
He is rather unduly severe on the single letter of
Keats which he quotes; but that was his way, and
it is after all only a justifiable rhetorical *reculade*, with
the intent to leap upon the maudlin defenders of the
poet as a sort of hero of M. Feydeau, and rend them.
The improvement of the mere fashion, as compared with
the fantasticalities of the *Friendship's Garland* period, is
simply enormous.   And the praise which follows is
praise really in the grand style—praise, the style and
quality of which are positively rejoicing to the heart
from their combination of fervour and accuracy, from
their absolute fulfilment of the ideal of a word shockingly misused in these latter days, the word Appreciation.   The personal sympathy which Mr Arnold
evidently had with Gray neither makes nor mars
here; all is purely critical, purely literary.   And yet
higher praise has never been given by any save the
mere superlative-sloppers of the lower press, nor juster
criticism meted out by the veriest critical Rhada-
manthus.   Of its scale and kind, this, I think, is the
most perfect example of Mr Arnold's critical power,
and it is so late that it shows that power to have
been not merely far off exhaustion, but actually, like
sound old wine, certain to improve for years to come.
   In the seven years that were left to him after the
publication of the *Byron*, Mr Arnold did not entirely

confine himself to the service of his only true mistress Literature. But he never fell again so completely into the power of Duessa as he had fallen between 1867 and 1877. His infidelities were chiefly in the direction of politics, not of religion or irreligion, and they were of a less gay and frivolous character than those of a generally similar kind in earlier dates. They were partly devoted to the change which has brought it about, that, while during the third quarter of the century the Conservatives were in power, though on three different occasions, yet in each for absolutely insignificant terms, in the fourth Mr Gladstone's tenure of office from 1880 to 1885 has been the only period of real Liberal domination. But although he dealt with the phenomenon from various points of view in such articles as " The Nadir of Liberalism," the " Zenith of Conservatism," and so forth, it was chiefly, as was natural at the time, in relation to Ireland that he exercised his political pen, and enough has been said about these Irish articles by anticipation above. *Discourses in America*, the result of his lecturing tour to that country in 1883-84, and the articles on Amiel, Tolstoi, and Shelley's Life, which represent his very last stage of life, require more particular attention.

The *Discourses in America*, two of them specially written, and the other, originally a Cambridge "Rede" discourse, recast for the Western Hemisphere, must always rank with the most curious and interesting of Mr Arnold's works : but the very circumstances of their composition and delivery made it improbable, if not impossible, that they should form one of his best. These circumstances were of a kind which reproduces itself frequently in the careers of all men of any public distinction. In his days of comparative obscurity, or in some position of "greater freedom and less responsibility," even when he ceases to be obscure, a man deals faithfully, but perhaps a little flippantly, with this or that person, thing, nation, subject, doctrine. Afterwards he is brought into a relation with the person or nation, into a position as regards the thing, subject, or doctrine, which necessitates, if not exactly a distinct recantation in the humiliating sense attached to the Latin, yet a more or less graceful and ingenious palinode in the more honourable one which we allow to the Greek equivalent and original. Mr Arnold could never be lacking in grace or in ingenuity; but he certainly had, in his earlier work, allowed it to be perfectly visible that the world of American politics, American manners, American institutions and ways generally, was not in his eyes by any means a world all of sweetness or all of light.

His sense of the ludicrous, and his sense of art, alike precluded even the idea of a clumsy apology, and though, as was to be expected, the folk of the baser sort who exist everywhere may not have been pleased with his Discourses, the people of the United States generally did not owe him or show him any grudge for being frank and consistent as well as polite. The subjects were selected and grouped with great skill.

"Numbers" dealt with the burning question of democracy, which must ever be uppermost—or as nethermost not less important—in a republic ; and dealt with it after the more moderate, not the extremer form, of that combination of literature and politics which Mr Arnold had always affected. "Literature and Science," the middle discourse, attacked a question which, so far as the nationality of his audience was concerned, had nothing burning about it, which the lecturer was singularly well qualified to treat from the one side, and which is likely to retain its actuality and its moment for many a day and year, perhaps many a century. "Emerson," the last, descended from generalities to the consideration of a particular subject, at once specially American and specially literary. It would have been hard indeed to exhibit better composition in the grouping of the subjects as regards their classes, and criticism may be defied to find better examples of each class than those actually taken.

It is not clear that quite such high praise can be given to the execution, and the reason is plain : it was in the execution, not in the composition and scheme, that the hard practical difficulties of the task came in. Long harnessed official as he was, and preacher as he was, in his critical character, of Law, Order, Restraint, Mr Arnold was both too much of an Englishman and too much of a genius not to be ill to ride with the curb. And, save perhaps in "Literature and Science" (which was not at first written for an American audience at all), the pressure of the curb—I had almost said of the twitch —is too often evident, or at least suggested. This especially applies to the first, the longest, the most ambitious, and, as its author would say, most "nobly serious" of the three. There are quite admirable things in "Numbers"; and the descant on the worship of the great goddess Aselgeia, and its effect upon France, is not only nobly serious from the point of view of morality, but is one of Mr Arnold's best claims to the title of a political philosopher, and even of a political prophet. But it is less easy to say that this passage appears to be either specially in place or well composed with its companions. Perhaps the same is true of the earlier part, and its extensive dealings with Isaiah and Plato. As regards the prophet, it is pretty certain that of Mr Arnold's hearers, the larger number did not care to have Isaiah spoken about in that particular manner, while some at least of the rest did not care to have him spoken about at all. Of the philosopher, it is equally safe to say that the great majority knew very little, and that of the small minority, some must have had obstinate questionings connected with the appearance of Plato as an authority on the moral health of nations, and with the application of Mr Arnold's own very true and very noble doctrine about Aselgeia. In fact, although the lecture is the most thoughtful, the most serious in part, the most forcible, and the truest of all Mr Arnold's political or social discourses, yet it shares with all of them the reproach of a touch of desultory dilettantism.

The others, at least equally interesting in parts, are much better as wholes. The opening of the "Emerson," with its fond reminiscence of Oxford, is in a vein which Mr Arnold did not often work, but which always yielded him gold. In the words about Newman, one seems to recognise very much more than meets the ear — an explanation of much in the Arnoldian gospel, on something like the principle of revulsion, of soured love, which accounts for still more in the careers of his contemporaries, Mr Pattison and Mr Froude. He is less happy on Carlyle—he never was very happy on Carlyle, and for obvious reasons — but here he jars less than usual. As for Emerson himself, some readers have liked Emerson better than Carlyle at first, but have found that Carlyle "wears" a great deal better than Emerson. It seems to have been the other way with Mr Arnold ; yet he is not uncritical about Emerson himself. On Emerson's poetry he is even, as on his own principles he was, perhaps, bound to be, rather hypercritical. Most of it, no doubt, is not poetry at all ; but it has "once in a hundred years," as Mr O'Shaughnessy sang, the blossoming of the aloe, the star-shower of poetic meteors. And while, with all reverence, one is bound to say that his denying the title of "great writer" to Carlyle is merely absurd—is one of those caprices which somebody once told us are the eternal foes of art—he is not unjust in denying that title to Emerson. But after justifying his policy of not "cracking up" by still further denying his subject the title of a great philo-

sophic thinker, he proceeds to find a pedestal for him
at last as a friend and leader of those who would "live
in the spirit." With such a judgment one has no fault
to find, because it must be in all cases an almost purely
personal one. To some Gautier, with his doctrine of

> " Sculpte, lime, cisèle,"

as the great commandment of the creative artist, has
been a friend and leader in the life of the spirit : to
Mr Arnold he was only a sort of unspiritual innkeeper.
To Mr Arnold, Maurice de Guérin, with his second-
hand Quinetism, was a friend and leader in the life of
the spirit ; others scarcely find him so. "This is this
to thee and that to me."

The third (strictly the middle) piece fortunately
requires no allowances, and suffers from no drawbacks.
"Literature and Science" is an apology for a liberal
education, and for a rationally ordered hierarchy of
human study, which it would be almost impossible to
improve, and respecting which it is difficult to think
that it can ever grow obsolete. Not only was Mr
Arnold here on his own ground, but he was fighting
for his true mistress, with the lance and sword and
shield that he had proved. And the result is like
that of the fortunate fights of romance : he thrusts
his antagonists straight over the crupper, he sends
them rolling on the ground, and clutching its sand
with their fingers. Even Mr Huxley, stoutest and
best of all the Paynim knights, never succeeded in

wiping off this defeat; and it is tolerably certain that no one else will. The language of the piece is unusually lacking in ornateness or fanciful digression; but the logic is the strongest that Mr Arnold ever brought to bear.

The three last essays we have mentioned, apart from the pathetic and adventitious interest which attaches to them as last, would be in any case among the best of their author's, and their value is (at least, as it seems to me) in an ascending scale. To care very much for that on Count Tolstoi is not easy for those who are unfashionable enough not to care very much for the eloquent Russian himself. Nothing is satisfactory that one can only read in translations. But Mr Arnold, in whom a certain perennial youthfulness was (as it often, if not always, is in the chosen of the earth) one of his most amiable features, seems to have conceived a new *engouement* for this new and quaintly flavoured Russian literature. Had he lived longer, he probably would have sung us something in a cautionary strain; just as it can never be sufficiently regretted that he did not live long enough to handle Ibsenism. And it would have been very particularly pleasant to hear him on those *Memoirs of a Mongol Minx* (as they have been profanely called), which are assigned to the great Marie Bashkirtseff; or on those others of the learned She-Mathematician, who waited with a friend on a gentleman and suggested that he should marry *one* of them, no matter which, and lead both about.

But the mixture of freshness, of passion, and of regard
for conduct in Count Tolstoi could not but appeal to
him ; and he has given us a very charming *causerie*
on *Anna Karenina*, notable — like O'Rourke's noble
feast—to

> " Those who were there
> And those who were not,"—

to those who have read the book itself, and to those
who have not yet found time to read it.

I cannot plead much greater affection for the lucu-
brations of Amiel than for Count Tolstoi's dealings
with that odd compound of crudity and rottenness,
the Russian nature ; but Mr Arnold's " Amiel " is admirable.   Never was there a more "gentlemanly cor-
rection," a more delicate and good-humoured setting
to rights, than that which he administers to Amiel's
two great panegyrists (who happened to be Mr Arnold's
own niece and Mr Arnold's own friend).   On subjects
like Maya and the "great wheel" it would almost
be impossible to conceive, and certainly impossible to
find, a happier commentator than Mr Arnold, though
perhaps in the regions of theology he had a private
Maya, a very Great Wheel, of his own.   The firmness
with which he rebukes the maunderings of the Gene-
vese hypochondriac—of whom some one once unkindly
remarked that he was not so much intoxicated with
Idealism as suffering from the subsequent headache—
is equalled by the kindness of the dealing ; and the
quiet decision with which he puts his fine writing in

its proper place is better still. Nobody could call Mr Arnold a Philistine or one insensible to *finesse*, grace, *sehnsucht*, the impalpable and intangible charm of melancholy and of thought. And his comments on Amiel's loaded pathos and his muddled meditation are therefore invaluable. Nor is he less happy or less just in the praise which, though not the first, he was one of the first to give to by far the strongest side of Amiel's talent, his really remarkable power of literary criticism.

But the best wine was still kept for the very last. It will have been observed in these brief sketches of his work that, since his return to the fields of literature proper, Mr Arnold had drawn nearer to the *causerie* and farther from the abstract critical essay,—that he had taken to that mixture of biography, abstract of work, and interspersed critical comment which Sainte-Beuve, though he did not exactly invent it, had perfected, and which somebody, I think, has recently described as "intensely irritating." Well! well! pearls, as we all know, are irritating to certain classes of consumers. He had from the first done this well, he now did it consummately. That he took occasion, in the paper on Shelley's life which appeared in the *Nineteenth Century* for January 1888, to repeat his pet heresy about Shelley's poetry, matters nothing at all. It is an innocent defiance, and no attempt whatever is made to support it by argument. The purpose of the essay is quite different. Already, some years before, in his

article on Keats, Mr Arnold had dealt some pretty
sharp blows both at the indiscretion of a certain class
of modern literary biographers, and at the pawing and
morbid sentimentality of the same persons or others.
He had a new and a better opportunity in the
matter he was now handling, and he struck more
strongly, more repeatedly, and with truer aim than
ever.   From the moment of its appearance to the
present day, this piece has been an unceasing joy to
all who love literature with a sane devotion.   Its composition is excellent ; it selects just the right points,
dwells on them in just the right way, and drops them
just when we have had enough.   In mere style it
yields to nothing of its author's, and is conspicuously and
quite triumphantly free from his repetitions and other
mannerisms.   No English writer — indeed one may
say no writer at all — has ever tempered such a blend
of quiet contempt with perfect good-humour and perfect
good-breeding.   Dryden would have written with an
equally fatal serenity, but not so lightly ; Voltaire
with as much lightness, but not nearly so much like a
gentleman — which may also be said of Courier.
Thackeray could not have helped a blaze of indignation—honest and healthy, but possibly just *plusquam-*
artistic—at the unspeakable persons who think that
by blackening the unhappy Harriet they can whiten
Shelley.   And almost any one would have been likely
either to commit the complementary error of being too
severe on Shelley himself, or, if this were avoided, to

underlie the charge of being callous and unsympathetic.
Every one of these rocks, and others, Mr Arnold has
avoided; and he has left us in the piece one of the
most perfect examples that exist of the English essay
on subjects connected with literature. In its own
special division of *causerie* the thing is not only
without a superior, it is almost without a peer; its in-
sinuated or passing literary comments are usually as
happy as its censure of vital matters, and even the above-
referred-to heresy itself gives it a certain piquancy. Ill
indeed was the fate that took its author away so soon
after the completion of this little masterpiece; yet
he could not have desired to leave the world with a
better diploma-performance, lodged as an example of
his actual accomplishment.

We must now return, for the last time unfortunately,
to the narrative of biographical events. December
1877 furnishes, in some letters to his sister, evidence
that he was increasingly "spread" (as the French
say quaintly) by notices of parties and persons—Mr
Disraeli and Mr Gladstone, Mr Huxley and Mr Ruskin.
One is glad to hear of the last-named that the writer
"is getting to like him"—the passages on the author
of *Modern Painters* in the earlier letters are certainly
not enthusiastic—and that "he gains much by his
fancy being forbidden to range through the world of
coloured cravats." This beneficial effect of evening
dress is not limited to Mr Ruskin, and is so well expressed that one only wishes Mr Arnold had let his

own fancy range more freely in such epistolary criticisms of life. We hear that Mr J. R. Green "likes the Reformation and Puritanism less the more he looks into them," again a not uncommon experience—and that Mr Stopford Brooke is deriving much edification from the review of his *Primer*. The next year continues the series of letters to M. Fontanès, and gives a pleasant phrase in one to another sister, Mrs Cropper. "My poems have had no better friends in their early and needy days than my own sisters"—wherein Mr Arnold unconsciously quotes *Goblin Market*, "there is no friend like a sister." Later, Mr Freeman is dashed off, *à la manière noire*, as "an ardent, learned, and honest man, but a ferocious pedant." 1879 yields a letter to Miss Arnold, expressing the intention to send the Wordsworth book of selections to M. Scherer, and beg him to review it, which request resulted in one of the very best, perhaps *the* very best, of that critic's essays in English Literature. Mr Arnold is distressed later at Renan's taking Victor Hugo's poetry so prodigiously *au sérieux*, just as some of us have been, if not distressed, yet mildly astonished, at Mr Arnold for not taking it, with all its faults, half seriously enough. Geist, the dachshund, appears agreeably, with many other birds and beasts, in a May letter of this year, and botany reinforces zoology in a later one to Mr Grant Duff.

1880 is at first less fertile, but gives an amusing account of a semi-royal reception of Cardinal Newman

at the Duke of Norfolk's in May, and a very interesting
series of letters from Pontresina in the autumn.   Fortunately for us Mrs Arnold was not with him, and we
profit by his letters to her.   In one of them there is
a very pleasing and probably unconscious touch.
"Rapallo [the Duchess of Genoa's husband] smokes
the whole evening : *but I think he has a good heart.*"
And later still we have the curious and not uncharacter-
istic information that he is reading *David Copperfield* for
the first time (whence no doubt its undue predomin-
ance in a certain essay), and the description of Burns
as "a beast with splendid gleams," a view which has
been fully developed since.   On February 21, 1881,
there is another interview, flattering as ever, with Lord
Beaconsfield, and later he tells M. Fontanès, "I never
much liked Carlyle," which indeed we knew.   The
same correspondent has the only references preserved
to Dean Stanley's death ; but the magnificent verses
which that death produced make anything else superfluous.   They appeared in the first number of the *Nineteenth Century* for 1882, when New Year's Day gives
us a melancholy prediction.   If "I live to be eighty
[*i.e.*, in some three years from the present moment],
I shall probably be the only person in England who
reads anything but newspapers and scientific publications."   Too gloomy a view, let us hope ; yet with
something in it.   And a letter, a very little later, gives
us interesting hints of his method in verse composition,
which was to hunt a Dictionary (Richardson's) for good

but unusual words—Théophile Gautier's way also, as it happens, though probably he did not know that.

These later letters contain so many references to living people that one has to be careful in quoting from them; but as regards himself, there is of course no such need of care. That self-ruthlessness which always prevented him from scamping work is amazingly illustrated in one of October 1882, which tells how he sat up till five in the morning rewriting a lecture he was to deliver in Liverpool, and got up at eight to start for the place of delivery. Let us hope that a champagne luncheon there — "chiefly doctors, but you know I like doctors" — revived him after the night and the journey. And two months later he makes pleasant allusion to "that demon Traill," in reference to a certain admirable parody of *Poor Matthias.* He had thought Mr Gladstone "hopelessly prejudiced against" him, and was proportionately surprised when in August 1883 he was offered by that Minister a pension of £250 for service to the poetry and literature of England. Few Civil List pensions have been so well deserved. But Mr Arnold, as most men of his quality would have been, was at once struck with the danger of evil constructions being put by the baser sort on the acceptance of an extra allowance from public funds by a man who already had a fair income from them, and a comfortable pension in the ordinary way to look forward to. Mr John Morley, however, and Lord Lingen, luckily succeeded in quieting his scruples, and only the very basest sort grumbled. The great advantage, of course, was that it enabled him to retire, as soon as his time was up, without too great loss of income.

A lecturing tour to America was already planned, and October 7, 1883 is the last date from Cobham, "New York" succeeding it without any; for Mr Arnold had the reprehensible and, in official persons, rare habit of very constantly omitting dates, though not places. The St Nicholas Club, "a delightful, poky, dark, exclusive little old club of the Dutch families," is the only place in which he finds peace. For, as one expected, the interviewers made life terrible. These American letters are interesting reading enough, but naturally tend to be little more than a replica of similar letters from other Englishmen who have done the same thing. As has been quite frankly admitted here, Mr Arnold never made any effort, and seldom seems to have been independently prompted, to write what are called "amusing" letters: he merely tells a plain tale of journeys, lectures, meals, persons, scenery, manners and customs, &c. Chicago seems to have vindicated its character for "character" by hospitably forcing him to eat dinner and supper "on end," and by describing him in its newspapers as "an elderly bird pecking at grapes on a trellis." The whole tour, including a visit to Canada, lasted nearly five months, and brought—not the profit which some people expected, but—a good sum, with wrinkles as to more if the experiment were repeated. And when he came back to England, the lectures were collected and printed.

In February 1885 we have, addressed to his eldest daughter, then married and living in America, a definition of "real civilisation" as the state "when the world does not begin till 8 P.M. and goes on from that till 1 A.M., not later." This is, though doubtless jestful, really a *point de repère* for the manners of the later nineteenth century as concerns a busy man who likes society. In the eighteenth, and earlier in the nineteenth, men as busy as Mr Arnold practically abstained from "the world" except quite rarely, while "the world" was not busy. The dachshunds come in for frequent mention.

On a Sunday in May of this year comes the warning of "a horrid pain across my chest," which, however, "Andrew Clark thinks [wrongly, alas!] to be not heart" but indigestion. The *Discourses in America*, for which their author had a great predilection, came out later. In August the pain is mentioned again; and the subsequent remark, "I was a little tired, but the cool champagne at dinner brought me round," is another ominous hint that it was *not* indigestion. Two of the most valuable of all the letters come in October, one saying, "I think Oxford is still, on the whole, the place in the world to which I am most attached" ["And so say all of us"]; the other, after some notice of the Corpus plate, telling how "I got out to Hinksey and up the hill to within sight of

the Cumnor firs.   I cannot describe the effect which
this landscape always has upon me : the hillside with
its valleys, and Oxford in the great Thames valley
below."   And this walk is again referred to later.   He
was pleased by a requisition that he should stand yet
again for the Poetry Professorship, though of course
he did not accede to it.   And at the beginning of
winter he had a foreign mission (his last) to Berlin,
to get some information for the Government as to
German school fees.   He was much lionised, and seems
to have enjoyed himself very much during his stay, the
Crown Princess being specially gracious to him.

Nor was he long in England on his return,
though long enough to bring another mention of the
chest pain, and an excellent definition of education
—would there were no worse !—" Reading five pages
of the Greek Anthology every day, and looking out all
the words I do not know."   In February 1886 he
was back again investigating the Swiss and Bavarian
school systems ; and that amiable animal-worship of
his receives a fresh evidence in the mention and
mourning of the death of " dear Lola " (not Montès,
but another ; in short, a pony), with a sigh for " a *mèche*
of her hair."   The journey was finished by way of
France towards the end of March.   At Hamburg Mr
Arnold was " really [and very creditably] glad to have
had the opportunity of calling a man Your Magnificence," that being, it seems, the proper official style
in addressing the burgomaster.   And May took him

back to America, to see his married daughter and divers old friends. He remained there till the beginning of September, improving, as he thought, in health, but meeting towards the close an awkward bathing accident, which involved no risk of drowning, but gave him a shock that was followed by a week or two of troublesome attacks of pain˙ across the chest. There is very much in the letters of the time about the political crisis of 1886. His retirement from official work came in November, and the letters are fuller than ever of delight in the Cobham landscape.

But the warnings grew more frequent, and we know that long before this he had had no delusions about their nature. Indeed, it is doubtful whether he had ever had any, considering the fact of the malady, which had, as he says in a singularly manly and dignified *commentatio mortis* dated January 29, 1887, struck down his father and grandfather in middle life long before they came to his present age. He "refuses every invitation to lecture or make addresses." The letters of 1887, too, are very few, and contain little of interest, except an indication of a visit to Fox How; while much the same may be said of those, also few, from the early months of 1888. The last of all contains a reference to *Robert Elsmere*. Five days later, on April 15, a sudden exertion, it seems, brought on the fatal attack, and he died. He had outlived his grand climacteric of sixty-three (which he had thought would be "the end as well as the climax") by two years and three months.

CHAPTER VI.

CONCLUSION.

THE personal matters which usually, and more or less gracefully, fill the beginning of the end of a biography, are perhaps superfluous in the case of a man who died so recently, and who was so well known as Mr Matthew Arnold. Moreover, if given at all, they should be given by some one who knew him more intimately than did the present writer. He was of a singularly agreeable presence, without being in the sense of the painter's model exactly "handsome"; and in particular he could boast a very pleasant and not in the least artificial smile. Some artificiality of manner was sometimes attributed to him, I think rather unjustly; but he certainly had "tricks and manners" of the kind very natural to men of decided idiosyncrasy, unless they transcend all mere trick, after the fashion which we know in Scott, which we are sure of, without knowing, in Shakespeare. One of these Mr George Russell glances at in the preface to the *Letters*, a passage which I read with not a little amusement, because I could

confirm it from a memory of my only conversation
with Mr Arnold.   He had been good-humouredly ex-
postulating with me for overvaluing some French poet.
I forget at the distance of seventeen or eighteen years
who it was, but it was not Gautier.   I replied in some
such words as, "Well ; perhaps he is not very important in himself, but I think he is ' important *for us*,'
if I may borrow that."   So he looked at me and said,
"*I* didn't write that anywhere, did I ? "   And when I
reminded him that he had told us how Sainte - Beuve
said it of Lamartine, he declared that he had quite
forgotten it.   Which might, or might not, be Socratic.

But I should imagine that the complaints of his
affectations in ordinary society were as much exaggerated as I am sure that the opposite complaints of the
humdrum character of his letters are.   Somebody
talks of the "wicked charm " which a popular epithet
or nickname possesses, and something of the sort
seems to have hung about "The Apostle of Culture,"
"The Prophet of Sweetness and Light," and the rest.
He only deserved his finical reputation inasmuch as
he was unduly given to the use of these catch-words,
not because he in any undue way affected to "look
the part " or live up to them.   And as for the letters,
it must be remembered that he was a very busy man,
with clerical work of the official kind enough to disgust
a very Scriblerus ; that he had, so far as the published
letters show us, no very intimate friend, male or (still
better) female, outside his own family ; and further, that

the degeneration of the art of letter-writing is not a
mere phrase, it is a fact. Has any of my readers many
—or any—correspondents like Scott or like Southey,
like Lamb or like FitzGerald, like Madame de Sévigné
or like Lady Mary? He is lucky if he has. Indeed,
the simplicity of the *Letters* is the very surest evidence
of a real simplicity in the nature. In the so-called best
letter-writers it may be shrewdly suspected that this
simplicity is, with rare exceptions, absent. Scott had
it; but then Scott's genius as a novelist overflowed
into his letters, as did Southey's talent of universal
writing, and Lamb's unalterable quintessence of quaint-
ness. But though I will allow no one to take pre-
cedence of me as a champion of Madame de Sévigné,
I do not think that simplicity is exactly the note of
that beautiful and gracious person ; it is certainly not
that of our own Lady Mary, or of Horace Walpole,
or of Pope, or of Byron. Some of these, as we know,
or suspect with a strength equal to knowledge, write
with at least a sidelong glance at possible publication ;
some with a deliberate intention of it ; all, I think,
with a sort of unconscious consciousness of "how it
will look" on paper. Of this in Mr Arnold's letters
there is absolutely no sign. Even when he writes to
comparative strangers, he never lays himself out for a
"point" or a phrase, rarely even for a joke. To his
family (and it should be remembered that the immense
majority of the letters that we possess are family letters)
he is naturally more familiar, but the familiarity does

not bring with it any quips or gambols. Only in the
very early letters, and chiefly in those to Wyndham
Slade, is there any appearance of second thought, of
" conceit," in the good sense. Later, he seems to have
been too much absorbed in his three functions of official,
critic, and poet to do more than shake hands by letter
and talk without effort.

But if he, as the phrase is, " put himself out " little
as to letter-writing, it was by no means the same in
those other functions which have been just referred to.
In later years (it is Mr Humphry Ward, I think, who
is our sufficient authority for it) poetry was but occasional amusement and solace to him, prose his regular
avocation from task - work ; and there is abundant
evidence that, willingly or unwillingly, he never allowed
either to usurp the place of the vocation which he had
accepted. Not everybody, perhaps, is so scrupulous.
It is not an absolutely unknown thing to hear men
boast of getting through their work somehow or other,
that they may devote themselves to *parerga* which they
like, and which they are pleased to consider more
dignified, more important, nearer the chief end of man.
And from the extremely common assumption that other
people, whether they confess this or not, act upon it,
one may at least not uncharitably suppose that a much
larger number would so act if they dared, or had the
opportunity. This was not Mr Arnold's conception of
the relations of the hired labourer and the labour which
gains him his hire. Not only does he· seem to have

performed his actual inspecting duties with that exact punctiliousness which in such cases is much better than zeal, but he did not grudge the expenditure of his art on the requirements, and not the strict requirements only, of his craft. The unfitness of poets for business has been often enough proved to be a mere fond thing vainly invented ; but it was never better disproved than in this particular instance.

Of the manner in which he had discharged these duties, some idea may be formed from the volume of *Reports* which was edited, the year after his death, by Sir Francis Sandford. It would really be difficult to imagine a better display of that "sweet reasonableness," the frequency of which phrase on a man's lips does not invariably imply the presence of the corresponding thing in his conduct. It would be impossible for the most plodding inspector, who never dared commit a sonnet or an essay, to deal with his subject in a way showing better acquaintance with it, more interest in it, or more business-like abstinence from fads, and flights, and flings. Faint and far-off suggestions of the biographer of Arminius may, indeed, by a very sensitive reader, be discovered in the slightly eccentric suggestion that the Latin of the Vulgate (of which Mr Arnold himself was justly fond) should be taught in primary schools, and in the rather perverse coupling of "Scott and Mrs Hemans." But these are absolutely the only approaches to naughtiness in the whole volume. It is a real misfortune that the nature of the subject should make readers of the book unlikely to be ever numerous ; for it supplies a side of its author's character nowhere else (except in glimpses) provided by his extant work. It may even be doubted, by those who have read it, whether "cutting blocks with a razor" is such a Gothamite proceeding as it is sometimes held to be. For in this case the blocks are chopped as well as the homeliest bill-hook could do it ; and we know that the razor was none the blunter. At any rate, the ethical document is one of the highest value, and very fit, indeed, to be recommended to the attention of young gentlemen of genius who think it the business of the State to provide for them, and not to require any dismal drudgery from them in return.

But the importance of Mr Arnold to English history and English literature has, of course, little or nothing to do with his official work. The faithful performance of that work is important to his character ; and the character of the work itself colours very importantly, and, as we have seen, not perhaps always to unmitigated advantage, the nature of his performances as a man of letters. But it is as a man of letters, as a poet, as a critic, and perhaps most of all as both combined, that he ranks for history and for the world.

A detailed examination of his poetic performance has been attempted in the earlier pages of this little book, as well as some general remarks upon it ; but we may well find room here for something more general still. That the poet is as much above the prose-writer in rank as he is admittedly of an older creation, has always been held ; and here, as elsewhere, I am not careful to attempt innovation. In fact, though it may seem unkind to say so, it may be suspected that nobody has ever tried to elevate the function of the prose-writer above that of the poet, unless he thought he could write great prose and knew he could not write great poetry. But in another order of estimate than this, Mr Arnold's poetic work may seem of greater value than his prose, always admirable and sometimes consummate as the latter is, if we take each at its best.

At its best—and this is how, though he would himself seem to have sometimes felt inclined to dispute the fact, we must reckon a poet. His is not poetry of the absolutely trustworthy kind. It is not like that of Shelley or of Keats, who, when their period of mere juvenility is past, simply cannot help writing poetry ; nor is it, on the other hand, like that of Wordsworth, who flies and flounders with an incalculable and apparently irresponsible alternation. It is rather—though I should rank it far higher, on all but the historic estimate, than Gray's—like that of Gray. The poet has in him a vein, or, if the metaphor be preferred, a spring, of the most real and rarest poetry. But the vein is constantly broken by faults, and never very thick ; the spring is intermittent, and runs at times by drops only. There is always, as it were, an effort to get it to yield freely, to run clear and constant. And—again as in the case of Gray—the poet subjects himself to a further disability by

all manner of artificial restrictions, struggles to comply
with this or that system, theories, formulas, tricks. He
will not "indulge his genius." And so it is but rarely
that we get things like the *Scholar-Gipsy*, like the *Forsaken Merman*, like the second *Isolation ;* and when we
do get such things there is sometimes, as in the case of
the peroration to *Sohrab and Rustum*, and perhaps the
splendid opening of *Westminster Abbey* and *Thyrsis*, a
certain sense of parade, of the elaborate assumption of
the singing-robe. There is too seldom the sensation
which Coleridge unconsciously suggested in the poem
that heralded the poetry of the nineteenth century.
We do not feel that

> "The fair breeze blew, the white foam flew,
>   The furrow followed free "—

that

> "We were the first that ever burst
>   Into that silent sea ; "

but that a mighty launch of elaborate preparation is
taking place, that we are pleased and orderly spectators
standing round, and that the ship is gliding in due
manner, but with no rush or burst, into the sea of
poetry. While elsewhere there may be even the sense
of effort and preparation without the success.

But, once more, a poet is to be judged first by his
best things, and secondly by a certain *aura* or atmos-
phere, by a nameless, intangible, but sensible quality,
which, now nearer and fuller, now farther and fainter,
is over his work throughout. In both respects Mr

Arnold passes the test. The things mentioned above and others, even many others, are the right things. They do not need the help of that rotten reed, the subject, to warrant and support them ; we know that they are in accordance with the great masters, but we do not care whether they are or not. They sound the poetic note ; they give the poetic flash and iridescence ; they cause the poetic intoxication. Even in things not by any means of the best as wholes, you may follow that gleam safely. The exquisite revulsion of the undertone in *Bacchanalia*—

> " Ah ! so the silence was,
> So was the hush ; "

the honey-dropping trochees of the *New Sirens ;* the description of the poet in *Resignation ;* the outburst—

> " What voices are these on the clear night air ? "

of *Tristram and Iseult ;* the melancholy meditation of *A Summer Night* and *Dover Beach*, with the plangent note so cunningly yet so easily accommodated to the general tone and motive of the piece,—these and a hundred other things fulfil all the requirements of the true poetic criticism, which only marks, and only asks for, the *differentia* of poetry.

And this poetic moment—this (if one may use the words, about another matter, of one who wrote no poetry, yet had more than all but three or four poets), this " exolution, liquefaction, transformation, the kiss

of the spouse, and ingression into the divine shadow"
which poetry and poetry alone confers upon the fit
readers of it—is never far off or absent for long together in Mr Arnold's verse. His command of it is
indeed uncertain. But all over his work, from *The
Strayed Reveller* to *Westminster Abbey*, it may happen
at any minute, and it does happen at many minutes.
This is what makes a poet : not the most judicious
selection of subject, not the most studious contemplation and, as far as he manages it, representation of
the grand style and the great masters. And this is
what Mr Arnold has.

That his prose, admirable as it always is in form and
invaluable as it often is in matter, is on the whole
inferior to his verse, is by no means a common opinion,
though it was expressed by some good judges both during his life and at the time of his death. As we have
seen, both from a chance indication in his own letters
and from Mr Humphry Ward's statement, he took very
great pains with it ; indeed, internal evidence would be
sufficient to establish this if we had no positive external
testimony whatsoever. He came at a fortunate time,
when the stately yet not pompous or over-elaborated
model of the latest Georgian prose, raised from early
Georgian "drabness" by the efforts of Johnson, Gibbon,
and Burke, but not proceeding to the extremes of any
of the three, was still the academic standard ; but when
a certain freedom on the one side, and a certain grace
and colour on the other, were being taken from the

new experiments of nineteenth-century prose proper. Whether he or his contemporary Mr Froude was the greatest master of this particular blend is a question which no doubt had best be answered by the individual taste of the competent. I should say myself that Mr Froude at certain moments rose higher than Mr Arnold ever did; nothing of the latter's can approach that magnificent passage on the passing of the Middle Ages and on the church-bell sound that memorises it. And Mr Froude was also free from the mannerisms, at times amounting to very distinct affectation, to which, in his middle period more especially, Mr Arnold succumbed. But he did not quite keep his friend's high level of distinction and *tenue*. It was almost impossible for Mr Arnold to be slipshod—I do not mean in the sense of the composition-books, which is mostly an unimportant sense, but in one quite different; and he never, as Mr Froude sometimes did, contented himself with correct but ordinary writing. If his defect was mannerism, his quality was certain manner.

The most noticeable, the most easily imitated, and the most doubtful of his mannerisms was, of course, the famous iteration, which was probably at first natural, but which, as we see from the *Letters*, he afterwards deliberately fostered and accentuated, in order, as he thought, the better to get his new ideas into the heads of what the type-writer sometimes calls the "Br*u*tish" public. That it became at times extremely teasing is beyond argument, and I should be rather afraid that Prince Posterity will

be even more teased by it than we are, because to him
the ideas it enforces will be, and will have been ever
since he can remember, obvious and common-place
enough.   But when this and some other peccadillos
(on which it is unnecessary to dwell, lest we imitate the
composition - books aforesaid) were absent or even
moderately present, sometimes even in spite of their
intrusion, Mr Arnold's style was of a curiously fascinating
character.   I have often thought that, in the good sense
of that unlucky word "genteel," this style deserves it
far more than the style either of Shaftesbury or of
Temple ; while in its different and nineteenth-century
way, it is as much a model of the "middle" style,
neither very plain nor very ornate, but "elegant," as
Addison's own.   Yet it is observable that all the three
writers just mentioned keep their place, except with
deliberate students of the subject, rather by courtesy or
prescription than by actual conviction and relish on the
part of readers : and it is possible that something of
the same kind may happen in Mr Arnold's case also,
when his claims come to be considered by other generations from the merely formal point of view.   Nor can
those claims be said to be very securely based in respect
of matter.   It is impossible to believe that posterity will
trouble itself about the dreary apologetics of undogmatism
on which he wasted so much precious time and energy;
they will have been arranged by the Prince's governor
on the shelves, with Hobbes's mathematics and Southey's
political essays.   " But the criticism," it will be said,

"*that* ought to endure." No doubt from some points of view it ought, but will it? So long, or as soon, as English literature is intelligently taught in universities, it is sure of its place in any decently arranged course of Higher Rhetoric; so long, or as soon, as critics consider themselves bound to study the history and documents of their business, it will be read by them. But what hold does this give it? Certainly not a stronger hold than that of Dryden's *Essay of Dramatic Poesy*, which, though some of us may know it by heart, can scarcely be said to be a commonly read classic.

The fact is—and no one knew this fact more thoroughly, or would have acknowledged it more frankly, than Mr Arnold himself — that criticism has, of all literature that is really literature, the most precarious existence. Each generation likes, and is hardly wrong in liking, to create for itself in this province, to which creation is so scornfully denied by some; and old critics are to all but experts (and apparently to some of them) as useless as old moons. Nor can one help regretting that so long a time has been lost in putting before the public a cheap, complete, handy, and fairly handsome edition of the whole of Mr Arnold's prose. There is no doubt at all that the existence of such an edition, even before his death, was part cause, and a large part of the cause, of the great and continued popularity of De Quincey; and it is a thousand pities that, before a generation arises which knows him not, Mr Arnold is not allowed the same chance. As it is, not a little of his work has never been reprinted at all; some of the rest is difficult of access, and what there is exists in numerous volumes of different forms, some cheap, some dear, the whole cumbersome. And if his prose work seems to me inferior to his poetical in absolute and perennial value, its value is still very great. Not so much English prose has that character of grace, of elegance, which has been vindicated for this, that we can afford to lay aside or to forget such consummate examples of it. Academic urbanity is not so universal a feature of our race— the constant endeavour at least to "live by the law of the *peras*," to observe lucidity, to shun exaggeration, is scarcely so endemic. Let it be added, too, that if not as the sole, yet as the chief, herald and champion of the new criticism, as a front-fighter in the revolutions of literary view which have distinguished the latter half of the nineteenth century in England, Mr Arnold will be forgotten or neglected at the peril of the generations and the individuals that forget or neglect him.

Little need be added about the loss of actual artistic pleasure which such neglect must bring. Mr Arnold may never, in prose, be read with quite the same keenness of delight with which we read him in poetry; but he will yield delight more surely. His manner, except in his rare "thorn-crackling" moments, and sometimes even then, will carry off even the less agreeable matter; with matter at all agreeable, it has a hardly to be exaggerated charm.

But it is in his general literary position that Mr Arnold's strongest title to eminence consists. There have certainly been greater poets in English : I think there have been greater critics. But as poet and critic combined, no one but Dryden and Coleridge can be for a moment placed beside him : the fate of the false Florimel must await all others who dare that adventure. And if he must yield — yield by a long way — to Dryden in strength and easy command of whatsoever craft he tried, to Coleridge in depth and range and philosophical grasp, yet he has his revenges. Beside his delicacy and his cosmopolitan accomplishment, Dryden is blunt and unscholarly; beside his directness of aim, if not always of achievement, his clearness of vision, his almost business-like adjustment of effort to result, the vagueness and desultoriness of Coleridge look looser and, in the literary sense, more disreputable than ever. Here was a man who could not only criticise but create; who, though he may sometimes, like others, have convicted his preaching of falsity by his practice, and his practice of sin by his preaching, yet could in the main make practice and preaching fit together. Here was a critic against whom the foolish charge, "You can break, but you cannot make," was confessedly impossible—a poet who knew not only the rule of thumb, but the rule of the uttermost art. In him the corruption of the poet had not been the generation of the critic, as his great predecessor in the two arts, himself secure and supreme in both, had scornfully said. Both faculties had always existed, and did always exist, side by side in him. He might exercise one more freely at one time, one at another; but the author of the *Preface* of 1853 was a critic, and a ripe one, in his heyday of poetry, the author of *Westminster Abbey* was a poet in his mellowest autumn of criticism.

And yet he was something more than both these things, more than both of these at once. But for that unlucky divagation in the Wilderness, his life would have been the life of a man of letters only as far as choice went, with the duties of no dishonourable profession superadded. And even with the divagation it was mainly and really this. To find parallels for Mr Arnold in his unflinching devotion to literature we must, I fear, go elsewhere than to Dryden or to Coleridge, we must go to Johnson and Southey. And here again we may find something in him beyond both, in that he had an even nobler conception of Literature than either. That he would have put her even too high, would have assigned to her functions which she is unable to discharge, is true enough; but this is at least no vulgar error. Against ignoble neglect, against stolid misunderstanding, against mushroom rivalry, he

championed her alike. And it was most certainly from
no base motive. If he wanted an English Academy, I
am quite sure it was not from any desire for a canary
ribbon or a sixteen-pointed star. Yet, after Southey
himself in the first half of the century, who has done so
much for letters *quâ* letters as Mr Arnold in the second?
His poems were never popular, and he tried no other of
the popular departments of literature. But he wrote,
and I think he could write, nothing that was not literature, in and by the fact that he was its writer. It has
been observed of others in other kinds, that somehow
or other, by merely living, by pursuing their own arts
or crafts whatever they were, they raised those arts
and crafts in dignity, they bestowed on them as it were
a rank, a position. A few—a very few—at successive
times have done this for literature in England, and Mr
Arnold was perhaps the last who did it notably in ours.
One cannot imagine him writing merely for money, for
position, even for fame—for anything but the *devoir*
of the born and sworn servant of Apollo and Pallas.
Such devotion need not, of course, forbid others of
their servants to try his shield now and then with
courteous arms or even at sharps—as he tried many.
But it was so signal, so happy in its general results,
so exactly what was required in and for England at
the time, that recognition of it can never be frank
enough, or cordial enough, or too much admiring.
Whenever I think of Mr Arnold it is in those own

words of his, which I have quoted already, and which I quoted to myself on the hill by Hinksey as I began this little book in the time of fritillaries—

> " Still nursing the unconquerable hope,
> Still clutching the inviolable shade "—

the hope and shade that never desert, even if they flit before and above, the servants and the lovers of the humaner literature.

INDEX.

THE END.